IN PRAISE OF
OSCAR ROMERO: PROPHET OF HOPE

"A compelling portrait with rare authenticity, *Oscar Romero* skillfully takes us beyond the controversy to encounter the humble pastor who simply tried to respond to God's call to shepherd his people, even at the cost of his life."

— Marie Paul Curley, FSP,
co-author, *Saints Alive! The Faith Proclaimed*
and *Saints Alive! The Gospel Witnessed*

"A highly-readable and well-documented portrait of a man of God who . . . was a shepherd of his people and a seeker of the justice and truth of God."

— Alicia C. Marill, D.Min., Associate Professor of Theology,
Director of Doctor of Ministry Program, Barry University

OSCAR
ROMERO

OSCAR
ROMERO

PROPHET OF HOPE

Roberto Morozzo della Rocca

Foreword by Hosffman Ospino, PhD

Preface by Andrea Riccardi

BOOKS & MEDIA

Boston

Library of Congress Control Number: 2015944954

CIP data is available.

ISBN 10: 0-8198-5466-2

ISBN 13: 978-0-8198-5466-7

Originally published in Italian as *Oscar Romero: La Biografia* by Roberto Morozzo della Rocca, © 2015 Edizioni San Paolo s.r.l. Piazza Soncoino 5 - 20092 Cinisello Balsamo (Milano), Italy. www.edizionisanpaolo.it.

Translated by Michael J. Miller

Special thanks to Maria Teresa Pompeii and Carmen Christi Pompeii, FSP, for additional assistance.

Cover design by Rosana Usselmann

Cover photo: corbis.com/Leif Skoogfors'; background: istockphoto.com/© filipe-frazao

First North American Edition, 2015

Published by Pauline Books & Media, 50 Saint Paul's Avenue, Boston, MA 02130-3491

Printed in the U.S.A.

www.pauline.org

Pauline Books & Media is the publishing house of the Daughters of St. Paul, an international congregation of women religious serving the Church with the communications media.

1 2 3 4 5 6 7 8 9   19 18 17 16 15

Contents

Foreword

The Witness of Archbishop Oscar Romero

 The beauty of the Christian experience is that God's Holy Spirit constantly moves the hearts of those called to be followers of Jesus Christ to witness the truth of the Gospel in the here and now of our lives. It is exactly where we are, in the continuum of history, sharing the joys and hopes of those who live with us while accompanying them in their grief and anxieties, that Christian life unfolds. Although every Christian is to live this same experience to the fullest, there are those whom the Church remembers with special love because through their lives we learn something special about the unending depths of God's divine mystery. We remember them as disciples, witnesses, saints.

On May 23, 2015 the Church celebrated the witness of Archbishop Oscar Romero from El Salvador in the ceremony of his beatification. That very same day I intentionally finished reading the present biography, written by Professor Roberto Morozzo della Rocca, and wrote this foreword. Doing so on this particular day afforded me the opportunity to participate in the experience of *being, feeling*, and *thinking* with the Church in a very unique way. These verbs, as Professor Morozzo della Rocca shares throughout his book, were defining for Archbishop Romero during his life as a man who deeply loved the Church.

For Romero, being, feeling, and thinking with the Church meant faithfulness to his vocation to being an authentic Christian disciple and to the ecclesial community within which he actively lived his witness. Such fidelity was expressed consistently through a special love for the Scriptures and the Church's Tradition. This is more than evident in the many homilies, pastoral letters, and other documents he wrote throughout his life. Without a doubt, Romero was a man of the Church. His fidelity was further realized through a sincere love for the people of El Salvador who during his time experienced the hardships of political corruption and extreme violence. Romero stood up firmly to affirm the values of the Gospel in a context where life, truth, and justice were blatantly dismissed by several sectors of the Salvadoran society. He walked as a man of faith and an advocate alongside the people of El Salvador, particularly the poor and the most vulnerable. Without a doubt, Romero was a man of the Church.

Romero's faithfulness ultimately led him to his martyrdom. As a contemporary martyr he speaks not only to the people of El Salvador or the Latin American communities, but also to the entire Church. The archbishop speaks loudly about the pastors that God's people longs for, pastors who are in intimate communion with the

Lord Jesus, who love the Church, and who understand the people they serve; pastors who inspire, pastors who, in the words of Pope Francis, "take on the smell of the sheep" (*Evangelii Gaudium*, 24). Romero's voice resounds in the hearts of the Christian community with an invitation to denounce the cultures of death in our midst and announce the truth of the Gospel with prophetic voice. In Romero, the words of Pope Paul VI find fulfillment: our world is more willing to listen to witnesses than to teachers, and if it listens to teachers, it is because they are witnesses (see *Evangelii Nuntiandi*, 14). During his life many listened to Romero; many more continue to listen to him after his death.

It is fascinating to observe how Romero's actions and words have inspired numerous interpretations about the life of this Latin American archbishop, his convictions, commitments, and even his influences. Some of those interpretations, in fact, seem to have gotten in the way of officially advancing Romero's canonization process for several years. Yet we seem to be beyond that impasse. This is where the work of historians and researchers helping us to understand Romero as a man in his time, living in a particular context, is more than welcomed. Comprehensive biographies of Romero, like this one written by Professor Morozzo della Rocca, and current efforts to organize and disseminate Romero's writings are gifts to the ecclesial community.

Of course, there will be many more interpretations of who Romero was and what he said. This is the power of the witness of those Christian disciples whose lives taught us more about the unending depths of God's divine mystery. Romero was a man of his time, and from a historical perspective it is good to have clarity about the conditions in which he lived as well as the reasons he made specific decisions inspired by his faith. Yet Romero is also a man of our time because he belongs to the same people for whom he cared so much as a pastor: the people of God. As Pope John Paul II repeated: "Romero is ours." He belongs to the poor and the afflicted because he loved them with a sincere heart. He belongs to the Church because every time the Christian community searches for inspiration to live out its faith, Romero stands tall in the cloud of witnesses reminding us that it is possible—in fact essential—to feel, to think with the Church (*Sentire Cum Ecclesia*), as the archbishop martyr's episcopal motto read.

May the reading of this biography of Archbishop Romero be an invitation to learn more about his life and thought. May it also inspire us to be ever more mindful about the millions of people in the world today who live in circumstances similar to the people of El Salvador during the time of Romero. Finally, may our hearts be moved to remember and support the many pastoral leaders— bishops, priests, deacons, sisters, catechists, missionaries, and countless lay evangelizers—whose hearts, like Romero's, are moved by the Holy Spirit to witness the truth of the Gospel as they stand for life, truth, and justice.

HOSFFMAN OSPINO, PhD

Boston, May 23, 2015
Archbishop Oscar Romero's Beatification

Preface

This book by Roberto Morozzo della Rocca is important because of its subject matter: the life of *Monseñor*
Oscar Arnulfo Romero, Archbishop of San Salvador in
Central America. While he was celebrating Mass on
March 24, 1980, he was killed by death squads connected with the
right-wing Salvadoran regime. He was sixty-two years old. The book
is also important because its author is a historian recognized as an
authority for his great insight and seriousness. Roberto Morozzo
della Rocca's historical research on Archbishop Romero (in this and
other writings) allowed him to reconstruct the true image of the
assassinated prelate. This image had either been covered by many
layers of polemics and ideologies, or it had been turned into a partisan banner. We must remember the decisive contribution that the
author's research has made toward the reconstruction of the historical truth about Romero and toward the slow, laborious clarification
of his process of beatification, which reached a positive conclusion

only with the pontificate of Pope Francis. Morozzo della Rocca's study was important for Romero's cause of beatification, in which it was essential to elucidate the richness and complexity of his character as a Latin American Christian and a Catholic bishop.

The failure to recognize Romero's "martyrdom," evident in the lack of progress in his beatification process, was a serious problem for the Church in Central America and all of Latin America. She was a mother who did not acknowledge the blood shed by one of her sons who had lived for her. Romero's episcopal motto reveals the meaning of his life: *"Sentir con la Iglesia."* "To think with the Church." But why was the martyrdom of this bishop not acknowledged? It was because of the tenacious opposition of some Latin American Catholics and bishops who considered him an ideological, mindlessly-progressive figure who had been manipulated by groups of liberation theologians. This interpretation was reinforced by the fact that Romero's name had become a symbol of the Latin American left, who held him up as a "revolutionary" icon. Morozzo della Rocca has demonstrated that Romero was a figure with great spiritual depth, not a politician but a pastor. History and historical research have their value, especially when they reconstruct the features of such a significant person.

Romero was a martyr. The Brazilian cardinal Lucas Moreira Neves, a prelate who worked in the Roman Curia, told me many years ago that he had met Romero at the Vatican on January 30, 1980. Romero was worried and said: "I will go back, but I will be killed; I do not know whether by the left or by the right." For the rest of Neves' life he carried a secret sorrow because of that interview, so much so that he attended the ceremonies in memory of the deceased archbishop. Romero knew that he would be killed in El Salvador but decided against staying in Rome for a while, as he had been invited to do. He returned to be a pastor among his people, even unto death. The failure to recognize his martyrdom had created, over the years, a kind of block in the depths of the Latin American ecclesial world. Although it was noticed only by more sensitive souls, it had an immense spiritual cost. With the beatification of Romero, not only has justice been done, but the splendor of the Church's motherhood of one of her best sons now shines forth.

Romero's story is a major episode in a country that went through terrible years. It shows how a bishop and a Church can be a haven of peace while everything is collapsing under the blows of senseless violence. In that difficult situation, Romero was a bishop and a friend of the poor. Indeed, the poor were his central concern, because he recognized in each poor person the mysterious presence of the Lord. Closeness to the poor was the compass of his life. As he preached on February 5, 1978: "There is one criterion for knowing whether God is close to us or far away: anyone who cares for the hungry, for the naked, for the poor, for those who have disappeared or been tortured, for the prisoner, for all suffering humanity, has God close to him."

Reading this book puts us in contact with one of the compelling sagas of the Church of the twentieth century. This story shows how a marvelous Christian achievement could come about in a small country, El Salvador, which was then unknown to most people. The story also reveals the secret but real face of a popular Catholicism of the "poor people" that is strong and resilient, and makes the reader more able to understand the national situation in which many political forces fought each other and dominated the life of El Salvador.

ANDREA RICCARDI

Founder of the Community of Sant'Egidio and Professor of Contemporary History at the University of Rome III in Rome, Italy

CHAPTER ONE

The First Fifty Years (1917–1967)

From Ciudad Barrios to Rome

 Oscar Romero was killed by a death squad on March 24, 1980, while he was celebrating Mass. For three years he had been Archbishop of San Salvador, the capital of El Salvador. For a long time he was a controversial figure. Romero was transformed by one political interest group into a revolutionary symbol, whereas the opposing party saw him as a Communist agitator. Only a day after his death a political myth sprang up about Romero, who was compared in messianic terms to individuals such as Camilo Torres [Restrepo], "Che" Guevara, or Salvador Allende. This led to a negative reaction in those who did not agree with those political figures.

The debates over Romero's reputation have been intense, especially during the civil war in El Salvador, which lasted from 1980 to 1992. A total of 80,000 people died out of a population of four million. Although as a public figure his actions were decisive for the fate of his country, today it is recognized that Romero was a man of the Church rather than a politician. His views and friendships far transcended the divisions between conservatives and progressives. As long as Romero was alive, El Salvador did not plunge into civil war. It began precisely in the wake of his death, for want of his efforts as a non-partisan peacemaker.

The beatification of Romero in the Catholic Church, following the acknowledgment of his martyrdom *in odium fidei* [hatred of the faith] comes at a time when many minds have been calmed. Now the tensions of the Salvadoran civil war and the bloody clash between military regimes and guerillas in Latin America have become things of the past. The sensational exploitation of the martyred bishop has dwindled. Throughout the world Romero receives honors that are impartially bestowed. Monuments, public squares, universities, airports, and hospitals have been named after him. He is the subject of books, films, and theatrical works.

But who was Romero, really?

Oscar Arnulfo Romero y Galdámez was born on August 15, 1917, in Ciudad Barrios. This town in eastern El Salvador is located at an altitude of 900 meters [3,000 feet], not far from the border with Honduras. His father, Santos Romero, was the local telegraph operator. Santos did not have a good disposition and was quick to anger. His small farm, the dowry of his mother Guadalupe de Jesús Galdámez, together with his house on the town square, helped the family to make a decent living. Two hired hands worked on the farm. Considering their surroundings, the Romeros could not be called poor. Like everyone in Ciudad Barrios, they had no electricity. The children slept together in common beds. The photos of the Romero family show faces with *mestizo* features, like the vast majority of Salvadorans.

At the age of four, Oscar was struck with polio. For a long time the disease affected his ability to move and to speak. The illness had long-range consequences on his character, accentuating his intelligence and thoughtfulness. An avid learner, Oscar was intrigued by words and their meanings. Being physically weak, he rarely played with boys his age. At school he showed no interest in mathematics, but he excelled in the Spanish language. Apart from suffering from polio, he had a happy childhood with his five brothers and two sisters (one of whom died in infancy).

Oscar's mother was very religious, but the same cannot be said of his father. Santos taught his children their prayers and the catechism, but his fellow townspeople remember him as not very fervent and somewhat insolent. Every evening, however, the Romero family recited the Rosary. Little Oscar liked to withdraw in prayer to the small village church and to get up at night to pray, according to the testimony of his younger brother Mamerto, who shared a bed with him. Mamerto, for his part, preferred to sleep.

At the age of thirteen, Oscar entered the minor seminary in San Miguel. From the town of one thousand with a cool climate in the middle of the mountains, Oscar went to the county seat, with twenty thousand inhabitants, on the hot plain. This decision was made because the mayor of the town, Alfonso Leiva, pointed Oscar out to Father Benito Calvo. He was the priest from San Miguel who regularly came up to Ciudad Barrios to perform the duties of pastor. Santos Romero had thought that Oscar might take up the carpenter's trade and had already sent him for an apprenticeship in a workshop. He agreed to let his son take another path, but then he had second thoughts and told the bishop of San Miguel that he no longer intended to support Oscar at the seminary. The bishop did not want to lose the boy and assumed part of the expense. Oscar also worked to pay his way at seminary. Among other things he spent one summer in a mine.

The boy liked the seminary. It was run in a paternal and humane spirit by the Claretian Fathers. The setting was provincial in the good sense, with attention to details, simple learning, and well-ordered discipline without excesses. Oscar liked living with his fellow students. He loved the idea of priesthood, preaching, music, and chant. He soon proved to be an outstanding speaker. Despite the modest setting, the seminarians were exhorted to give their best. The young Romero drew up and revised resolutions and plans for prayer, penance, and daily discipline—for personal sanctification, as eager seminarians everywhere used to do. The favorite devotions at the seminary were to the Virgin of Peace of San Miguel and to the Sacred Heart of Jesus. Romero would remain faithful to them for the rest of his life.

The Bishop of San Miguel, Juan Antonio Dueñas, wanted his two most promising seminarians, Oscar Romero and Rafael Valladares, to study in Rome. Rafael had been sent to Rome in 1934, and Romero joined him in October 1937. The two young Salvadorans, who shared a common life and a close friendship that would end only with the death of Valladares in 1961, lived at the Pontifical Latin American College in Rome. Both were ordained to the priesthood in Rome: Valladares on March 23, 1940, since he was four years older, and Romero on April 4, 1942.

Valladares was a young man with a fine mind and a severe, restless character. Social class meant a lot in El Salvador. Rafael, Bishop

Dueñas' nephew, was the son of rich landowners, unlike the other seminarians. For Romero, he was a difficult model to imitate. Although Rafael was used to winning first place, he was humble enough to wish Oscar well. Rafael showed sensitivity to social issues, was interested in current events, and talked with Oscar about them. He was clever and imaginative, whereas Oscar had a more systematic way of thinking.

In Romero's biography, the Roman years (1937–1943) are fundamentally important. "*Romanità*," or doing as the Roman clergymen do, was a decisive element in Romero's formation and later in his identity as a priest and a bishop. Romero belonged to the generation of clergymen that tried to reform the unfortunate—even calamitous—state of the Latin American clergy in regard to discipline and spirituality. One sign of this reform was the firm intention of the central See of Catholicism to imprint a more Roman character on the Latin American Church. This meant the formation of Church personnel who would overcome a certain provincialism, have a more universal sense of the Church, practice steadfast moral discipline, distinguish the spheres of Church and State, and distance themselves from politics so as to give priority to ecclesial and spiritual concerns. In a way, it was a matter of founding the Latin American Church anew, given the decadence of its educational institutions and the loss of the proper sense of the Church in relation to the rest of society. Centuries of the Spanish system of *Patronato* [1] [royal patronage] had led to confusion of the sacred and the secular. Madrid had excluded Rome from Latin America, and the States born of the Bolivarian revolution [in the early nineteenth

---

1. Under this system the kings of Spain had great influence in Church affairs in Latin America, including the appointment of bishops. —*Ed.*

century] would try to do the same, in order to keep the Church subject to the civil authority.

Romero studied at the Gregorian University, which was run by the Jesuits, as was the Pontifical Latin American College. As he became acquainted with and absorbed the spirituality of the Society of Jesus, he began to make an Ignatian retreat periodically. Romero himself says what they meant to him in a diary entry from 1972: "The exercises of Saint Ignatius [of Loyola] are a personal effort to put Christianity into practice. They are not the great general principles of revelation or of the magisterium, but personal conversation with God. 'I have seen God,' Jacob said. This must be my yearning: 'Speak to me, Lord.'"

Romero participated in the religious life of "Italian" Rome, as was usually the case with clerics who came to the city for their studies and formation. He served in parishes on the outskirts of Rome. A Mexican fellow student at the Latin American College would later remember Romero as follows:

> He was of average height, light-brown complexion, and firm bearing, like someone who is in no hurry because he knows that he will reach his goals. In dealing with others he appeared peaceful and calm.... From what I remember, his intelligence was above average. I would say that his literary style was elegant, with word usage and metaphors that gave grace and ease to his prose. When he read what he had written, the way he expressed himself gave his words greater life.... He was respectful of norms, devout, and concerned about his priestly formation in all its aspects. He knew how to make friends and we, who were already his friends, held him in high esteem because of his simplicity and his desire to be helpful.

During his stay in Rome, Romero developed an affectionate devotion to the pope, which he maintained for the rest of his life. He had a special veneration for Pius XI. Romero noted and admired the steadfastness of the man whom he called "the Pontiff of imperial stature" (*"Pontífice de talla imperial"*) for confronting totalitarian ideologies and regimes. The twenty-year-old Romero admired and internalized the model of a strong bishop, embodied by Pius XI. In later years Romero would rate the living example of Pius XI, whom he watched closely, as more important for his formation than the entire curriculum of his studies in Rome. To quote his own words, "In Rome I had to live through the drama of the Church facing the totalitarianisms of Hitler and Mussolini. I learned from the imperial Pius XI the boldness to confront those in power fearlessly and to tell them: 'As long as I am Pope, no one will laugh at the Church.' " In an article Romero wrote in 1963, he described the death of Pius XI, which occurred while the Pontiff was writing a "transcendental speech . . . meant to denounce the hypocritical attitude of the modern Neros who martyr the Church." "This is the pope whom I admire the most," Romero would say at the tomb of Pius XI in January 1980, during his last visit to Rome. He was well acquainted with that tomb. He had attended the burial of the deceased Pontiff on February 14, 1939: "We saw him close up: his pale face, the mouth already livid; we touched his right hand with an indescribable emotion." Pope Pius XII did not impress young Romero as much; he simply saw in him a pope suited to his time. In his heart only Pius XI was *"imperial."*

Rome confirmed and increased Romero's deference to the magisterium of the Church. He was particularly impressed by the solemn ceremonies that he attended. His studies were not geared to scholarly research but to formation, which consisted essentially of being in Rome. This was an absolute value in itself, more important than any scholarly achievements in his studies. Twenty years later Romero would observe:

The privilege of studying in Rome was valuable not so much for the scholarly aspect as for the moral support of a priestly education completed in the Roman setting. Rome is the most beautiful symbol and synthesis of the Church. Eternal Rome, while continuing to be the same through the centuries, takes on the historical characteristics that correspond to the individual personalities of the popes. It is a miracle of Providence: each pope embodies in his way of being the aspect that is most needed at that time in the life of the Church.

According to Romero, Rome itself prepared him for priestly life, as though its educational institutions were secondary:

> For a seminarian who is devotedly preparing for the demands of his vocation, what a splendid school it is to observe and experience a Rome that is displayed beneath the visible hand of God which is the Pope. . . . Roman spring has a mystery of ineffable sweetness; through the historic streets, by the light of dawn, the newly ordained priests go to celebrate their first Masses at the most famous altars in Christendom: the catacombs, the tomb of Saint Peter, of Saint Paul, [the Basilica of] Saint Mary Major, etc. And, all the fervor of the martyrs and pilgrims whose story is connected with those spiritual centers of attraction is revived in the soul that has just been consecrated.

The documentation on Romero's stay in Rome shows a young man fascinated by the city of the popes, who practiced self-denial, and is intent on his duties of study and religious piety. To put it simply, Romero wanted to be holy. He wrote to his mother once a month, continually emphasizing that he was journeying "toward perfection." Having no money to buy books, Romero copied by hand onto file cards the readings and thoughts that interested him. Most of these file cards, which he always kept, concerned spirituality, asceticism, and mysticism. It is not unusual for a seminarian to be interested in Christian perfection, but in Romero this interest was pronounced.

After he finished the usual studies in theology,[2] Romero wanted to specialize in the study of ascetical theology so as to earn a *laurea* degree. He did not have a chance to defend his thesis orally because of the wartime situation, which prompted him to return to his country. Romero later remembered those difficult days as follows:

> Europe and almost the entire world were in flames during World War II. Fear, uncertainty, and news of bloodshed, created an atmosphere of terror. At the Pio Latino, rations were smaller every day. The rector would go out searching for food and come back with pumpkins, onions, chestnuts, or whatever he could find hidden under his cape. Hunger caused many Italian seminaries to close. The Pío Latino had to confront the situation since all its resident students were from other countries; those who could return home faced a perilous journey. Those who stayed suffered from homesickness more than ever. Almost every night sirens announced air raids from the enemy and we had to run to the cellars. Twice these were more than just warnings and the Roman suburbs were riddled by horrible bombardments.

In August 1943 Romero left Rome, which had been under bombardment for several months. He made the long and difficult journey back to his country with Valladares. As passengers arriving in Cuba from Italy (a country allied with Germany), Romero and Valladares were suspected of espionage and imprisoned in a concentration camp. There they ran the risk of dying of starvation, hardships, and sickness. When they were recognized as clerics by a Cuban priest, the two men were first admitted to a hospital and then set free. They arrived in El Salvador in December 1943.

---

2. Romero was ordained in April 1942. —*Trans.*

Priest in San Miguel

Bishop Dueñas had died, and his successor as bishop of San Miguel was Miguel Angel Macado. In the spring of 1944, he appointed Romero pastor in Anamorós, a small, out-of-the-way village. After two months, however, the bishop called him back to be his secretary, a sign of his confidence in the young priest. Romero and Valladares, with their credentials from their studies in Rome, were a major investment for the diocese and were not destined for second-rate assignments. Romero also assumed responsibility for the city parish of Santo Domingo, which was being temporarily used as the cathedral. Since the bishop did not want to have a vicar general for the time being, Romero was also put in charge of the secretariat of the diocesan curia. He kept that job even when Valladares, in better health by then, was appointed vicar general. So Romero and Valladares went back to living side by side. Observing Romero's abilities day by day, the bishop was pleased with him and gave him more duties each year. Romero was a pastor, a spiritual director for men and women religious, the editor-in-chief of the diocesan weekly newspaper, the rector of the minor seminary, the president of the cathedral building commit-tee, the promoter of devotion to Our Lady of Peace, and a religion teacher. He was also a chaplain for Catholic Action, the Legion of Mary, the Honor Guard of the Most Blessed Sacrament, the Franciscan Third Order, the Apostleship of Prayer, the Knights of the Holy Sepulcher, the Cursillo Movement, the Christian Family Movement, and Alcoholics Anonymous.

Romero lived with his mother (until her death in 1961) and his sister Zaída, of whom he had been very fond since childhood. (His father had died in 1937, a few days before Romero left for Rome.) Who was the Romero of the years in the diocese of San Miguel? He was a man who pursued first and foremost an ideal of priestly life through constant prayer and recollection, the diligent performance of his spiritual and liturgical duties, frequent examinations of conscience, vigilance over his thoughts, disciplined activity, fasts, penances, and praying the Rosary. This was at the expense of the activist side of his character. Yet it was the spiritual basis that sustained his inclination to work. In his spiritual retreats he was strict, especially about solitude. The Claretian Fathers in San Miguel recall that every year he made a week-long retreat at their house to reflect and pray, which he would spend in absolute silence. He did not utter a word and did not even want to eat with others.

Romero's aspiration to reach "the dizzying heights of priestly dignity" did not mean that he lived his priesthood with superhuman assurance. Interiorly Romero waged a battle to reaffirm constantly the ideal to which he had been consecrated in Rome on April 4, 1942. In 1972 he noted the following about his "vocational decisions": "at my ordination: I was immature and not sure about celibacy. Other human perspectives: fear of life in some other profession, fear of what people might say. . . ." During retreats, Romero sometimes lists "sensuality" among the temptations that he had to combat, in the sense of fleeing persons and places that might stimulate him. "Sensuality" has a complex meaning for Romero: it is not only attraction to the opposite sex, but also the danger of "spiritual dissipation" and of "adopting middle-class ways," as well as the instinctive natural reluctance to offer one's life unconditionally to follow Christ. In any case, Romero had no dalliances unbefitting a Catholic priest. Nor did he doubt the fundamental motives for his "vocational decisions." He thought that his vocation was "certain and divine." He conscientiously rejected "the earthly motives" for it, and hoped for the help of God's grace to seek nothing but "the glory of God, the service of the Church, and my own salvation." He believed that celibacy, in his own case too, was a providential "sign of and incentive to charity . . . an extraordinary source of spiritual fruitfulness."

The faithful of San Miguel appreciated and loved him. Romero knew the mentality of the people and interpreted it wisely. Even the well-to-do families treated him affectionately. He was able to touch hearts in his preaching and personal conversation. The Romero of San Miguel was an accessible, generous man, charitable toward the poor. There are well-known incidents of goods and money that he gave to them when he could have used them for himself. In order to give the hungry something to eat, he himself sometimes fasted. He had to give up the administration of the parish because he was so generous that the funds quickly ran out. He founded an association of "Shoeshine Boys of San Miguel" and provided meals and lodging for them on parish premises. He created a youth oratory that taught catechism and also served as a trade school. He regularly visited the prisons, helped prostitutes to get off the street, and helped alcoholics to quit drinking. Every week he visited the sick at the hospital. He asked the diocesan branch of Caritas, which distributed food, to teach people about proper nutrition. He visited the rich, catechized them, and asked them to make donations for the poor. By evening in the confessional, he was so tired that he once assigned the penance: "Recite five pesos."

During his years in San Miguel, Romero was accused of "Communism" because he had criticized how the *cafetaleros* [coffee-growers] treated their workers. Some prominent figures, irked by his calls for the just distribution of goods as part of Catholic social doctrine, accused him of misappropriating funds. He was administrator of the offerings collected for the new cathedral, so they accused him of diverting some of the money to his personal use. He was even accused of stealing the jewels that adorned the statue of Our Lady of Peace. Although Romero was not scrupulous in managing worldly goods, he was innocent: money and jewels left him completely indifferent.

The clergy, who were more easy-going, considered him too demanding and criticized his severity. Jealousies can easily grow in the ecclesiastical world. Indeed, Romero was present everywhere, if only by the generosity with which he sought to respond to every request. One group of male religious asked the bishop to restrict his activities. Some priests said that he was a reactionary. They were annoyed by his claim that the priesthood should be understood as a daily martyrdom. Romero had no close friends among the clergy, except for Valladares. For this reason Bishop Machado did not choose Romero as his vicar general when Valladares left San Miguel to become auxiliary bishop in San Salvador (where he died prematurely in 1961). Some remarks Romero made about Valladares' years in San Miguel (1944–1956) can probably be applied to his own experience during those same years in that same setting, as if Romero were looking at his reflection in his friend's difficulties:

> In the curia of San Miguel and in his work for the seminary he was inspired solely by the honor of the diocese, which eclipsed all personal distinctions. [Valladares] used to say: "You must meditate on what should be done, and when you see what should be done it doesn't matter what people say about you." Someone once told him that he was excessively severe and dictatorial, and he replied: "Yes, I know that I have a dictatorial temperament, and if I had gone into politics perhaps I would have been a dictator. But there are good dictatorships, and especially in the Church we must not do things by half-measures." That firmness, however, which was feared by the obstinate and the proud, proved to be kind and welcoming to those who acknowledged their failings.

Romero's health was sometimes frail because he worked too much. In 1955 the bishop prescribed for him three months of compulsory vacation. Even then his health was the subject of gossip by hostile individuals. In his personal archive Romero kept a letter from 1964, written by a physician to the apostolic nunciature, which had heard rumors about him:

> I can tell you that Father Romero is not suffering from pulmonary tuberculosis. . . . Those who say that Father Romero is demented are lying about his condition. . . . Nor does Father Romero suffer from paralysis in any part of his body. Father Romero is a worthy priest, a great fighter who works tirelessly. No doubt this zeal for work results occasionally in a natural exhaustion, since any body subjected to such excessive work of that nature naturally grows tired and needs time to recuperate. This is why both personally and in my professional capacity I have required Father Romero to take a vacation, possibly outside the country.

Romero combined asceticism and activism according to a traditional, productive ideal of Christian perfection. He continued to make periodically the spiritual exercises of Saint Ignatius. He also associated with Opus Dei, whose founder, Josemaría Escrivá de Balaguer, he had met in 1955 during a trip to Europe. Romero admired Opus Dei for its fidelity to the Church, its commitment to work, and its "supernatural sense": traits he cultivated in his own life. Indeed, Romero prayed a great deal, felt prompted to action by his prayer, lavished serious efforts and determination on his work, and intended to be faithful to the Church at all costs. The periodicals he read—from *Ecclesia* to *L'ami du clergé*, from *La Civiltà Cattolica* to *L'Osservatore Romano*—were characterized by their indisputable fidelity to the magisterium, to Tradition, and to the universality of the Roman Catholic Church. Romero listened to Vatican Radio every day. He was not a modernizer. He always wore a cassock; first and foremost he cultivated his priestly identity, yet he understood the mentality of the people and he knew how to interpret it.

A Fighting Man

During his years in San Miguel, Romero did not flee from conflicts. He had adversaries whom he challenged and confronted. Romero's public courage was not apparent only in his years as archbishop. Among other things, he was a combative, polemical journalist, not out of a love for controversy, but because he identified with the style of a fighting, unyielding Catholicism.

Romero periodically attacked Communism. He studied the enemy and recognized analogies with Christianity, especially in the sincerity of its militant supporters and in their goal of the common good, but he disagreed with the Marxist plan of separating man from God: "Communism claims to create a new kind of people. . . . The specific trait of a human being is religiosity. . . . Without religion, he is no more than an animal. Well, then, this is what Communism claims: to uproot from him any religious sentiment." He mentioned economic reasons for the clash with Communism, in relation to private property, but he assigned only relative importance to it: "This is not the essential thing. The serious, decisive, unmistakable reason why Christianity will always be anti-Communist is above all the fact that Communism denies God, and Christianity affirms God."

Romero's attacks on Communism became less frequent as the Cold War subsided in the new international climate of the sixties, during the pontificate of John XXIII. Romero emphasized that the Second Vatican Council did not accept a proposal by three hundred bishops to condemn Communism. He deduced from this that the crucial question was a different one: the authenticity of Christianity, which by itself would frustrate the claims of Communism to authority. In 1967 Romero spoke about a "prudent, sincere dialogue" with the Communists to "edify the world" common to all. He unceasingly praised the *Ostpolitik*[3] of Paul VI, which was criticized by other Catholics whose anti-Communism prevailed over other considerations.

Romero also severely condemned the modern liberal State, Masonic influence on public life, and the reluctance of the authorities to accept the social doctrine of the Church. One might even say that, to Romero's way of thinking, Communism was a consequence of the mother of all heresies: the secularizing liberalism that has separated society from God. Freemasonry was influential in El Salvador from the 1930s to the 1950s. Romero censured the "depressing Masonic and liberal terms" in which the Spanish colonial period before independence was commonly described by the ruling class as "a yoke, slavery, and obscurantism." With his strong sense of history, Romero denied permission to use the cathedral for a celebration in honor of Gerardo Barrios, a liberal and a Mason, who from 1858 to 1863 had held the highest offices in the Salvadoran government. This decision drew criticism in local circles. Romero's birthplace, Ciudad Barrios, had been called Cacahuatique until 1913. Its name was changed specifically in honor of Gerardo Barrios, who had been born there one century before. Romero's judgment on the public figure was not mitigated by love of his hometown. Furthermore, Romero refused to allow a Christian burial for Masons. He attributed the misrule of the

---

3. *Ostpolitik* refers to Paul VI's policies regarding the Soviet Union and the Eastern European countries it controlled. —*Ed.*

country to the liberal and Masonic elements in the mentality and customs of the ruling classes. He commented on the national holiday in 1962:

> Which Fatherland? The one that our rulers serve, not to improve it but to enrich themselves? The one belonging to this lurid history of liberalism and Freemasonry, which essentially propose to degrade the people so as to manipulate them at their whim? The Fatherland of wealth distributed in the worst possible way, in which a brutal social inequality makes the vast majority of those born on their own soil feel like rejects and foreigners?

For the sake of the common good, Romero desired good relations between Church and State, and the state protection of morality. He had patriotic sentiments, while of course firmly upholding the priority of God over Caesar, which he often emphasized by repeating the Salvadoran expression: *"¡Primero Dios!"*[4] When the public authorities showed respect for the Church, Romero was almost moved by it. In 1967 an outgoing president of El Salvador took leave by quoting, among other things, *Pacem in Terris*.[5] Shortly afterward the new president cited *Populorum Progressio* by Paul VI, noting the Pope's vision of "the development of peoples." Romero took the occasion to enthusiastically assure those in government, in the name of Salvadoran Catholics, of "a patriotism that makes us the best servants of the common good of El Salvador." But in the opposite situation, Romero was not in awe of any civil authority. For him, the Church was a "supernatural

---

4. "God first!" —*Trans.*

5. This is Pope John XXIII's encyclical, *Pacem in Terris: On Establishing Universal Peace in Truth, Justice, Charity, and Liberty* from April 11, 1963. —*Trans.*

society" quite different in its reason for existing from "political society," and each of the two societies was independent and sovereign in
its proper sphere:

> Since the two societies govern the same people, at the same time,
> on the same soil, mixed problems tend to arise, which must be
> settled peaceably by means of concordats. But if at times "politics
> touches the altar," as Pius XI used to say, then that very fact will
> oblige the Church to touch politics in defense of the altar. In
> other words, the Church will not be concerned about the laws of
> the State, because that is not her province. But if someday the
> laws of the State trample the divine law, then the Church will
> condemn those laws and forbid Catholics to abide by them.

In 1964 the government accused Romero of interfering in political matters and threatened to haul him into court. The leaders were
alarmed by the rapid growth of support for the Christian Democratic
Party. But Romero was not intimidated. He defended his right "to
guide the people's consciences." He said that the government's "slanderous denunciation" was due to the influence of Freemasonry,
whose "incompatibility with a Catholic conscience" he reaffirmed.

In the local setting, too, Romero did not let the political authorities affect his ministry. In 1962 he clashed with the municipal
administration and the businessmen's association in San Miguel.
They wanted to schedule a carnival on November 21 to take advantage of the large crowds drawn by the local feast day of Our Lady of
Peace. He succeeded in getting the carnival postponed by three
days, but he could not prevent it. He deemed it a profane interference as well as a display of vulgar immorality. Year after year, he
continued to denounce the complicity of the authorities with the
"vice" and the "sensuality" of "dancing and dining in all the districts"
right after the festivities in honor of Our Lady, the patroness of El
Salvador.

In 1963 Romero organized a city-wide mission with the Claretians, Redemptorists, and "Mondo Migliore"[6] priests. Among other things he sought to bring about the regularization of de facto unions, which were rather widespread. The mayor did not cooperate, and Romero decided to celebrate religious weddings without waiting for civil weddings first. This action aroused the ire of the local administration and of the Masonic press. Romero countersued, and the litigation continued for a long time, involving even the national government. It became a philosophical question, a dispute about the primacy of the civil or the religious element in marriage. Romero declared that Colonel Sánchez Hernández, the Ministry of the Interior, had "a mentality of faded liberalism," despite "his education and European trimmings."

Romero constantly dreamed of an El Salvador ruled by Christian ideals. He expressed it in different terms at various stages in his life: Christian civilization, the coming of Christ the King, the kingdom of God on earth. The country's name, which was the name of Christ the Savior, left no doubt in his mind. Even the national capital, San Salvador, was a reminder of it. During his years in San Miguel, Romero lived in a city dedicated to an archangel, with districts that bore Christian names: *barrio de Concepción, barrio de la Cruz, barrio de la Merced, barrio del Calvario, barrio de San Felipe, barrio de San Francisco, barrio del Centro y del Patrón San Miguel, colonia Belén.* At the same time Romero knew that the Salvadoran people had been inadequately evangelized. He realized that the population was far from the Catholic ideals of morality, family, and

---

6. Founded by Father Riccardo Lombardi, SJ, in Italy after World War II, this association of priests, religious, and laity work for a better world by promoting peace and justice. —*Ed.*

social justice. It was no accident that he insisted on living the Ten Commandments. In 1947 the diocese of San Miguel had only twenty-one priests for 556,783 inhabitants. This meant that each priest had the care of 26,513 souls, if not more, given that not all the priests were involved in parish ministry. The Salvadoran province displayed, in miniature, the perennial paradox of Catholicism in Latin America, "the continent of hope." But in reality it could not provide for itself the personnel necessary for a thoroughgoing evangelization. Romero well knew these problems of the Church in Latin America and in his own country. But all this did not prevent him from proclaiming the Christian destiny of El Salvador. For him it was an incontrovertible fact that his country had a Catholic identity. At the same time he knew that he had much work to do if the Christian faith that he proclaimed was to be effective.

During his years in San Miguel, Romero recognized the social problems. As he put it, suitable laws were needed in regard to workers, fair wages, respect for labor contracts, and the redistribution of national resources. He worried about "divided and disgraced" families, women with children by various men, widespread alcoholism, prostitution, corruption, and rampant theft. The social issue reminded Romero above all of a need for conversion on the part of the rich, who had to be more compassionate and show greater respect for human dignity. In 1961 the seventieth anniversary of *Rerum Novarum* was celebrated. The encyclical, described as the "Magna Carta of the Church's social doctrine," appeared to Romero to be a "third way" between liberalism and socialism: "Liberalism had demonstrated its inability to resolve the acute problem; moreover it had even created it. Socialism offered remedies which instead were poisons that aggravated the situation." Romero asserted that Pope Leo's encyclical still had relevance, given the selfishness on the one side and the class hatred on the other. He also admonished the rich in words and warnings that would recur again and again during his years as archbishop. It was necessary to put *Rerum Novarum* into practice before it was too late:

> An Italian bishop advised the people of his diocese: "divest your-selves; if not, they will divest you." Which is to say: hasten to find a worthy solution to the acute social problem, which today is more unavoidable than ever. A solution in keeping with faith and reason, in accordance with social justice and Christian love. This is the solution that *Rerum Novarum* proclaims. . . . Otherwise God will allow a violent, hateful, brute-force solution to triumph, like a scourge.

Romero and the Second Vatican Council

In order to accentuate the stereotype of the traditionalist priest, some have maintained that Romero was upset by the innovations of the Second Vatican Council. But his writings and speeches from the sixties show no evidence of that claim. On the contrary, Romero was very enthusiastic about the Council. In the diocesan newspaper he published its documents, commented on them, and extolled them. It was not easy to understand Vatican II from afar in San Miguel. On the eve of the opening of the Council, Romero saluted it in the type of language he was accustomed to: "The Church's atti-tude in this solemn hour of the Ecumenical Council is identical to the vigorous gesture of the Archangel, who defends the rights of God against the forces of hell that wish to claim the conquests of technology in order to forge a world without God and against God." Romero greeted the Council with the language of the fifties, without the slightest inkling of the Council's new vocabulary. Like many council fathers in Saint Peter's Basilica, Romero gradually understood that the purpose of Vatican II was not to reaffirm dogmas and condemnations, but to help the Church address modern times. He arrived at this understanding through the interpretation and language of Paul VI. Romero wrote in 1964:

> In the Pope's voice there is a cry of hope. An immense hope, because it is the time for renewal. Let us not forget that we are in the age of the Ecumenical Council. "Renewal," the Church has cried, and no one will be able to stop this renewal because the Holy Spirit himself is blowing. We are in a time in which the Church is being renewed. It is not just a restoration of the Church's external prestige, which convinces no one, but a firm and open-minded renewal that makes the Church appear simpler and more biblical.

Romero knew that the new ideas of Vatican II were causing confusion. He dedicated himself to convincing the faithful of San Miguel of the goodness of the conciliar reforms:

> The laws about the eucharistic fast have changed; the schedules for Holy Week have been modified, and the altar for celebrating Mass is now positioned facing the people. Now you see that many Catholics are reading the Bible. The priests are talking about sociology and pastoral ministry. In view of this, many Catholics have become uneasy and wonder suspiciously whether they are not being asked to change their religion. . . . No, there is nothing to fear. Let them not confuse their habits with their religion. . . . The history of the Church is a history full of changes, because in every age the Church confronts new problems.

In any case the conciliar *aggiornamento* was not without a guide, as he wrote in 1965:

> The Church, then, is in an hour of *aggiornamento*, that is, of crisis in its history. And as in all *aggiornamenti*, two antagonistic forces emerge: on the one hand, a boundless desire for novelty, which Paul VI described as "arbitrary dreams of artificial renewals"; and

on the other hand, an attachment to the changelessness of the forms with which the Church has clothed itself over the centuries and a rejection of the character of modern times. Both extremes sin by exaggeration. Unconditional attachment to what is old hampers the Church's progress and restricts its "catholicity," which has both a geographical and a historical meaning, enabling it to be in tune with all civilizations and all eras. The boundless spirit of novelty is an imprudent exploration of what is uncertain, and at the same time unjustly betrays the rich heritage of past experiences.... So as not to fall into either the ridiculous position of uncritical affection for what is old, or the ridiculous position of becoming adventurers pursuing "artificial dreams" about novelties, the best thing is to live today more than ever according to the classic axiom: *think with the Church.* Practically speaking, this means unconditional attachment to the hierarchy. Because the Pope and the bishops are the men inspired by God for the *aggiornamento* of the Church in every hour of its history.

According to Romero, "the return to the Gospel was the characteristic, insistent note of Vatican II." He saw the Council as a pastoral event, which did not call into question dogma or the substance of the faith. Indeed, after the Council "more dogma than morality will be preached to the people, because morality is a consequence of faith and grace."

The Romero of the post-conciliar era had new worries. His striving for holiness was not diminished. His many commitments and responsibilities continued, taxing his strength to the utmost. But after over twenty years of priesthood, Romero felt the need for an interior renewal. The fervent aspirations and mental categories of his youth could not remain unchanged. He also noticed a tremendous change in the reality all around him because of Vatican II.

The Church was changing her forms, sensibilities, language. Romero followed in the wake of Vatican II; during those years he intensely studied its documents and their pastoral implications. He did not perceive the Council as a break—for Romero, the Church does not make breaks—but he did recognize its power to change. Romero noted the "climate of springtime that we breathe in this post-conciliar hour." His compass and guide was Paul VI, whom he praised as "the Pope of dialogue," "leader of peace in the world," "the pilgrim of friendship among peoples," "the new prophet of the development of peoples and of social justice," and "the genuine advocate of the poor against abuse by the rich." Romero also saw in Montini[7] the pope of the "eternal truth of the Gospel," of tradition, and of continuity with his predecessors. Yet Romero's main impression was of a new spirit of the papacy and of the Church.

Romero's personal diaries contain interesting entries for January 1966. He wrote them during his spiritual exercises in the "wonderful climate" of Planes de Renderos, on a height that escaped the heat of underlying San Salvador. It was Romero's first retreat in the post-conciliar period:

> The fundamental meditation on the Kingship of Christ [according to the Ignatian Exercises] coincides with three facts that promote *an extraordinary reform*: a) the post-conciliar period is demanding renewal throughout the Church, especially of priests; b) the arrival of *Monseñor* Graziano in San Miguel, who has such great hopes in me and who must know my secrets . . . ; c) and my 25th priestly jubilee in April. Above all, the second offers me the prospect of a possible change of setting, for which I must have an interior disposition of sanctification. Among my readings *The Diary of a Soul* by Pope John XXIII charmed me and taught me a lot. Above all, I am amazed at how he uses the same methods as

---

7. That is, Pope Paul VI. —*Ed.*

the spiritual exercises of Saint Ignatius, pious practices, devotion to the Sacred Heart of Jesus . . . which shows the efficacy of the method and demonstrates how little I correspond with grace. I read also the Pope's speeches and documents from that solemn conciliar hour.

For some time Romero had been seeing a psychologist in order to relieve the nervous tension resulting from his fatigue. He did so with the understanding of his confessor. The psychologist had summarized his character in the following terms: "obsessive-compulsive perfectionist." The doctor's suggestion was: "set another objective for my personality." This advice did not displease Romero. During the spiritual exercises he thought of Borromeo, who more than anyone else had helped to implement the Council of Trent: "It would be noble to have an *obsession for Christ*, actualizing it in *his post-conciliar Church*. That is, the obsession to be one of the saints that the Pope is calling for, one of the Charles Borromeos who want to collaborate to reflect in their life and work the face of Christ in his Church."

These words indicate how much Romero felt called by that historical moment of the Church. His life, however, as he himself noted, was shaken not only by the conciliar renewal but also by a change in the diocesan hierarchy. In 1965 Romero was the most active, most highly-educated and authoritative priest in San Miguel. Having studied in Rome, he had good relations with the apostolic nuncio, who asked him to draft speeches and consulted him about local ecclesiastical questions. Nevertheless his uneasy relations with the clergy of San Miguel impeded Romero's selection as successor of the elderly Bishop Machado. The latter asked the Holy See for an auxiliary bishop who would succeed him, while ruling out Romero as a candidate. In September 1965 it became known that the man destined for the See of San Miguel was Lawrence Graziano, a North

American prelate who had been auxiliary bishop in Santa Ana since 1961. He was four years younger than Romero. He officially succeeded Machado on January 10, 1968, but he had performed the duties of the ordinary from the time he arrived in the diocese.

Romero would have liked to have been Machado's successor. But he uttered not a word of recrimination about his failure to be appointed. He resolved to collaborate loyally with the new bishop. Graziano arrived in San Miguel directly from a working session of Vatican II and introduced the conciliar reforms in the diocese. Parish and presbyteral councils were formed, but Romero did not attend them. Until then he had been at the center of every movement and diocesan initiative. It was difficult for him to accept collegiality and to share responsibility with others for whom he did not always have great esteem. It was not that Romero opposed the new ideas of Vatican II. For someone of his mentality it was inconceivable to oppose ecclesial orthodoxy. Graziano's reform efforts upset him for personal reasons, not as a matter of principle. Graziano, who was originally from New York, had an informal style. He dressed casually even when he welcomed visitors, and, given the atmosphere in San Miguel, this was not the worst charge leveled at him by the old-style Catholics. It was natural for Graziano to delegate responsibilities among the various priests of the diocese, and Romero saw his duties decrease. He reacted by focusing his energies on places where his work was appreciated. On the eve of Graziano's arrival he had already started to collaborate with the apostolic nunciature in drafting speeches and opinions. He made himself available to such requests, which always continued to grow. Finally he left San Miguel.

The *Acts* of the Episcopal Conference of El Salvador (CEDES) recorded the appointment of Romero as secretary thereof on June 8, 1967. Soon after, the news spread in San Miguel, sparking some protests by the faithful. A committee in favor of "Romero in San

Miguel" called on the nuncio. Discontent with Graziano grew among the laity of the diocese of San Miguel, for they considered him responsible for sending Romero away from the city. Graziano defended himself in the diocesan newspaper with a kindly note about Romero, stating that the decision had been made by CEDES as a whole. Romero publicly thanked Graziano for "such courteous words of praise" and urged the faithful to show "obedience to the ecclesiastical authority" and to have a "sincere devotion to the unity of the Church."

CHAPTER TWO

"El obispo que van a tener es pastor"[1]

In the Capital

Starting in 1967, Romero had a new life in San Salvador. He resided at the spacious seminary of San José de la Montaña, which also housed the offices of the episcopal conference and of the archdiocese of San Salvador. With his habitual zeal Romero applied himself to his duties as secretary of CEDES. His job was to record minutes, to file papers in the archive,

---

1. "The bishop you are going to have is a pastor." —*Ed.*

to handle correspondence, and to draw up documents. His work was much appreciated. In addition, the Archbishop of San Salvador, *Monseñor* Chávez, asked him to perform some pastoral ministry in the archdiocese. Given his efficiency, the Episcopal Secretariat of Central America and Panama (SEDAC) also requested his services. In May 1968 Romero was appointed Executive Secretary of SEDAC, and from then on he had to attend its periodic meetings in Guatemala.

In 1970 Romero became a bishop. The appointment was foreseeable, given the tasks that he was performing and the high regard in which the nuncio and the other bishops held him. He was now fifty-three years old. A brother priest who had been a few years ahead of him in the seminary, the late Valladares, had become a bishop at the age of forty-three. Even so, Romero's episcopal appointment came about due to a specific circumstance. In the late sixties SEDAC wanted its secretary to be a bishop. Since no bishop in Central America was willing to take on this bureaucratic burden, it was decided to promote to the episcopate the efficient priest who was then serving as the secretary—Romero. SEDAC asked Chávez to establish a position for Romero in the Archdiocese of San Salvador, while leaving him time for duties outside the diocese. The nuncio communicated to Romero the news of his episcopal appointment on April 21, 1970. Romero recorded the circumstances as follows:

> April 21, 1970: The nuncio notifies me of the Pope's decision. I must respond tomorrow. . . .
>
> a) with regard to the basic problem: accept it as a sacrifice, expiation, take the correction seriously: flee the occasions [of sin], intense life of prayer and mortification.
>
> b) with regard to the temptation to triumphalism: see it as a serious responsibility, a service that is never easy, a work in the presence of God.

    c) with regard to the temptation to pusillanimity: see it as a
       work in God's sight, service and guidance for millions of
       souls. The Good Shepherd gives his life for his sheep.

During a retreat a few weeks later, Romero reconsidered the circumstances of his nomination and his first reactions: "Uncertain conscience, mixture of ambition, fear of not being qualified and of having to resign, a sense of penance and reparation. My God, what uncertainty! I feel that I accepted almost without having fully reflected. I am trying, however, to make my decision conscientiously and correctly."

Romero chose the episcopal motto: "Think with the Church." It had already been his way of life for a long time. It comes from the spiritual exercises of Saint Ignatius.

Even though he was now an auxiliary bishop, Chávez did not force Romero to work in the diocese. The archbishop knew that Romero lacked authority over the clergy, who thought his social and political views were too traditional. In this new context Romero was confronted with the same problem he had found in San Miguel: difficult relations with the diocesan clergy. The clergy of San Salvador did not care for Romero's appointment as auxiliary. Between 1967 and 1970, Romero had done little to curry favor with them. At the seminary where he lived, he led a very reserved and quiet life. He was intent on his duties, in keeping with his timid, very focused, and meticulous character. One could hear his typewriter clattering at all hours of the night. In the seminary he had no close friends except for a Jesuit, Father Rutilio Grande. The distrust of the clergy was reciprocated by Romero.

With the faithful, he was the same affable, generous Romero he had been at San Miguel. Over time his duties outside the diocese diminished. In late 1972 Romero completed his service as secretary of SEDAC. In June 1973 another secretary replaced him in CEDES.

Romero and Chávez had a good relationship. The two men understood each other in basic spiritual matters. Romero liked Chávez's people-oriented pastoral ministry and social inspiration. For his part, Chávez esteemed Romero for his priestly spirit and his untiring efforts. The archbishop guessed that Romero was a good pastor, despite the bureaucratic duties he had been assigned. When Romero became Bishop of Santiago de María in late 1974, Chávez surprised a priest of the small diocese by confiding in him, *"Esté seguro, el obispo que van a tener es pastor."*[2] Yet in his four years as auxiliary in San Salvador, Romero's work most often had ended in failure.

The story of the interdiocesan seminary had embittered him the most. CEDES had appointed him rector in August 1972. The seminary was run by a team of priests from various dioceses. Romero immediately found himself in conflict with the one responsible for discipline, Freddy Delgado, a priest of the diocese of San Vicente. He was rigid and stifling in his control of the seminarians' lives, but Romero was more indulgent and paternal. He considered it legitimate for the seminarians to leave the grounds for weekly unsupervised excursions. After Delgado expelled one seminarian and others left in protest, Romero sought to dismiss his colleague. Delgado left San José de la Montaña but obtained from CEDES the post of Secretary of the Conference, in Romero's place. Romero complained to his confreres in the episcopate about the hurried appointment, which did not observe the normal procedure. But Delgado was supported by his bishop, Pedro Aparicio.

The seminary faced major financial problems. Despite the relatively small number of residents, the palatial building still had to be maintained. To save on general expenses, Chávez moved the

---

2. "Be sure of it: the bishop you are going to have is a pastor." —*Trans.*

diocesan minor seminary to San José de la Montaña. But the Bishop of San Vicente, the above-mentioned Aparicio, decided to withdraw his seminarians, thus decreasing the financial contribution of his diocese. The seminary found itself so deeply in debt that it could not continue. A financial rescue was impossible, so in August 1973 CEDES decided to close the seminary. According to the preferences of the individual bishops, the seminarians were either sent abroad to study, or else returned to be tutored individually by their former Jesuit instructors, with the seminary officially closed.

In that disastrous incident Romero had made an enemy of Freddy Delgado, who as secretary of CEDES would be hostile to him in later years as well. Aparicio—with whom Romero had had conflicts in CEDES to the point that Romero had publicly called him a "liar"—had secretly come by night to remove the seminarians of the San Vicente diocese and take them elsewhere. Romero had overtaken him at the gate, and Aparicio had told him that he did not want his men to have "an extreme-right seminary formation." Aparicio was then thought to be a bishop with social sensitivities, but in reality he followed first and foremost the unpredictable promptings of his own ego. He did not even hesitate to clash with Chávez the "progressive," out of jealousy with regard to the archdiocese.

The story of the *Externado* San José was no less painful for Romero. The *Externado* was a university-level boarding school run by the Jesuits. At the school, the new orientation of the Salvadoran Jesuits who had gone over to liberation theology made itself felt. The Society of Jesus in El Salvador had also undergone a change of personnel. A group of "young Jesuits," enamored of political theology and no longer trained in Rome or in Spain but in Northern Europe, had outflanked the older members who had more moderate views. The young Jesuits became the preponderant element and took charge of the local governance of the Society. In the *Externado* they actively spread their leftist political ideas, as had also happened at the UCA, the Jesuit-run University of Central America. The upper-class, well-to-do families of the students at the *Externado* began to protest against the "politicized education." In May 1973 Romero published an editorial in the diocesan weekly newspaper *Orientación* entitled "Educación Liberadora pero Cristiana y sin Demagogia."[3] In it he criticized Latin American systems of education for being abstract, formalistic, and uncritical. He said they certainly needed a "liberating education," but added that none of this justified what was happening in those colleges that had no respect for the "old masters." This situation took advantage of the "innate generosity and restlessness of our young people in order to start them down the paths of demagogy and Marxism (and we do not use this word lightly; the works and writings themselves that are circulated at a certain college, with their manifestly Red origins, are what prompt us to use it)."

The parenthetical remark is said to have been added by a colleague at *Orientación*, but Romero adopted it as his own and signed the editorial. Did he imagine the consequences? Immediately the major Salvadoran newspapers, which had ties to the oligarchy, attacked the *Externado*, which was easily identifiable in Romero's editorial. They demanded repressive measures, all the more so now that the Church itself was denouncing the school in its official newspaper. Shortly before this the state university had been closed, and some professors who were accused of Communist subversion

---

3. This is translated as "An Education That Is Liberating but Christian and without Demagogy." —*Trans.*

had been expelled from the country. President Molina considered applying similar measures to the *Externado*. The Procurator General of the Republic started an investigation. "The problem of the *Externado*" became the subject of conversations and correspondence among Molina, the nuncio, Aparicio, various government ministries, and the Jesuits. The government intended to exploit the incident for its own advantage.

Romero received furious letters from the superior of the Jesuits in El Salvador, Miguel Francisco Estrada. He commanded Romero to retract his statements and to make "complete reparation," "publicly and immediately," threatening otherwise to take the field against him "personally." Romero avoided polemics with Estrada. He forwarded his letters to the nuncio and to CEDES, and both found them ill-mannered. In all the CEDES meetings during the summer of 1973, the Externado case topped the agenda. In El Salvador all the parties made public statements with explanations and corrections: the Jesuits, one bishop or another in his personal capacity, an investigative commission appointed by Chávez, the pro-government press, the courts, and members of the executive branch. Romero refrained from commenting on the polemical developments, and at the CEDES meetings he remained silent.

Romero the auxiliary bishop in the early seventies can be understood in the context of the pontificate of Paul VI, in the midst of the post-conciliar difficulties. Although a reformer, the Pope found himself left in the dust by the extreme innovators. He felt caught between the two passions of protest and traditionalism. He was concerned about finding the right balance for a Church that seemed to be listing to one side or the other. He was no longer the Paul VI of the well-organized conciliar project and of the hopeful sixties, the man of great symbolic gestures, the papal "expert on humanity" of the visit to the United Nations, the prophet of *Populorum*

Progressio. Nor was he then the Paul VI of the Holy Year and of *Evangelii Nuntiandi,* who would recover his confidence and momentum toward the end of his life.

The Paul VI that Romero regularly reported on in the periodicals he wrote for (*Orientación, La Prensa Gráfica, El Diario de Oriente*) was the sorrowful, discouraged, suffering man who felt betrayed by the innovators and thwarted by the conservatives, who wondered whether "the smoke of Satan" had entered the Church. Romero quoted Paul VI who denounced the "self-destruction" of the Church, wrought from within. Or else Romero noted the formula lamented by Paul VI, "The Church Without." This referred to a distorted reformist movement that would have liked to have a Church "without" holiness, authority, the cross, obedience, sacrifice, and so on. On other occasions Romero repeated the appeals of Paul VI not to make an "arbitrary and false interpretation of the Council" as if it had intended to shred tradition and change dogma.

At the same time, being faithful to the teaching Pope Paul VI articulated, Romero did not fail to praise "the sincere efforts to update" promoted by the Council and the Pope. He also emphasized other pronouncements of Paul VI that called for optimism and spoke about the "exuberant spring of the post-conciliar Church," new pastoral organizations to be proud of, the increase of the "social sense and of active charity," a greater diffusion of the Gospel, a "more acute sense of evangelical poverty," and an openness to "the positive values of the world." He also extolled the international synods of bishops, which Paul VI had convened, as events similar to Pentecost and that recalled the conciliar experience. Romero noted first that they were not to be interpreted as "a struggle between left and right, or a battle between liberals and conservatives." However, according to Romero, the different positions were useful in the synod debates: "pluralism and freedom of discussion" had confirmed "the fine aphorism which John XXIII had applied to recent times in the Church: *in necessariis unitas, in dubiis libertas, in omnibus caritas.*"[4]

Romero saw Paul VI as the great "Pope of Balance." In Romero's preaching and writing the idea of a crisis in the Church was copied from the teaching of Paul VI, as were the appropriate remedies, starting with personal conversion. During the sixties, Romero had taken the Council as a strong impetus to the internal reform and the renewal of the Church. In the early seventies, he experienced increasing difficulties to implement it. Amid contradictory opinions, he sought an equilibrium between the old and the new. "Tradition and Progress," he emphasized, go together. As auxiliary bishop of San Salvador, Romero was critical of the innovators who were guilty by their own admission of not knowing the historical and theological patrimony of centuries of Christian life. He accused them to their faces of immanentism, neo-modernism, sociologism, ambiguous prophecy, and of setting politics above religion and of tending to violence. At the same time, Romero's fidelity to Vatican II was undeniable. He continually quoted the conciliar documents in his talks and writings. The authors that he quoted in *Orientación* were not part of currents opposed to the spirit of the Council, but were theologians and bishops who believed in Vatican II: Karl Rahner, Marcos McGrath, Eduardo Pironio, Leo Suenens. In an intervention in 1972, Romero cited Suenens significantly:

> It is not uncommon to come across people who would like a clear, decisive break with the past, so as to start over from zero. And it is not uncommon to meet others who with systematic resistance oppose any form of renewal and adaptation, preferring an

---

4. This is translated as "in necessary things, unity; in doubtful things, freedom; in all things, charity." —*Trans.*

unchanging status quo. Although the first position is unfair and even childish, the second implies a lack of faith in the Church and in the presence and action of the Holy Spirit within it. And it can also include a strong, perhaps unconscious dose of fear of risk, egotism, or convenience. The conservatives—Cardinal Suenens says—frequently confuse Tradition with traditions, and the progressives confuse liberty with anarchy. The conciliar position is a position of integration, which brings about a vital synthesis of these two forces, Tradition and liberty.

An Auxiliary Bishop with His Own Ideas

In theological and ecclesiological questions, Auxiliary Bishop Romero was basically guided by the magisterium of Paul VI, which was sometimes cautious and restrained, at other times combative and bold. In general, he sought to follow the path being taken by the Church as it was articulated by Rome, by CEDES, and by Chávez. His organizational and intellectual duties obliged him to work in an institutional setting, far from the pastoral care of people. Romero was bound to tradition but was not a stubborn conservative. Romero appreciated modernity in practical matters. He enjoyed television, tape recordings, and radio programs. Later, as archbishop, he would gladly become a technician in his interviews on Radio YSAX, the diocesan radio station. But the fact that he liked technology was not the reason why he found conservatism too narrow. In a more essential way, Romero was open to the developments of history, to the understanding of the realities by which he measured his own efforts. He maintained that one must not idolize the past. In particular, Vatican II could not be called into question. If any priests showed nostalgia for the past, Romero admonished them. As much as he distrusted some extreme innovators, he could not bear reactionaries who were fixated on the past. He thought that was incompatible with the spirit of the Gospel and the magisterium of the Church.

Those were the years of liberation theology. In this regard Romero's position was clear. An acceptable theology of liberation was one that arrived at heavenly or "transcendent" realities, as Romero used to say, and was not exclusively concerned with earthly realities. The term *liberación* had to be understood correctly as *salvación*. Otherwise one ran the risk of having a merely political, demagogic, immanent, materialist liberation and of chasing after sociological theories and Marxist practices. According to Romero, the correct theology of liberation was that of Paul VI when he spoke about the necessity of "integral salvation." In Latin America, people commonly spoke about *liberación integral*. Romero liked to speak about the *salvación integral* of the human being as a whole, body and soul, with an earthly destiny and a heavenly destiny. For him, the "true liberation theology" was none other than "the eternal theology of salvation in Christ" who came to redeem us from sin.

This was not merely a question of vocabulary. Liberation theology asked Christians to put themselves into the heart of political life. In this sense the word *liberación* had to replace the word *salvación*. The latter traditional expression, "salvation," did have its disadvantages: salvation appeared to be solely the work of divine grace without human cooperation; it seemed to apply to the individual rather than society; it suggested a redemption that was more spiritual than temporal.

Romero had harsh words for the liberation theologians who, in his view, did not understand that true liberation was from sin and who furthermore relied on non-Christian ideologies. Those Catholics were seized by "a psychosis of rancorous prophetism." Their "prophetic denunciations" were "devoid of prophecy but full of politics." They misrepresented the figure of Christ, who is understandable only in "the truth of his cross": there was no such thing as a "guerrilla, Marxist Christ, the economist and politician." Nevertheless Romero sought to discern what good might be in the new post-conciliar theological currents. He was not against things just because they were new: "The theological development that we as Christians of our time must accept is the one which, for the noble task of dialogue with a world that is also evolving and needs Christian answers for its heightened sociopolitical mentality, emphasizes more than in the past the temporal, political, and social dimensions, without, however, obscuring eternal, spiritual, personal, and eschatological values."

According to Romero, the one who expressed liberation theology in a wise, balanced way was Eduardo Pironio. This Argentine bishop stood out from the rest of the Latin American bishops because of his erudition, meekness, and spirituality. He was a friend of Paul VI, who made him a cardinal in 1976. Romero became acquainted with Pironio at a plenary assembly of the Latin American bishops in Antigua, Guatemala, in 1970, shortly before his own episcopal consecration. He met him again at spiritual retreats in later years. He followed Pironio's public statements. Romero had in his small personal library six books by Pironio (with obvious signs of use, unlike the volumes by other proponents of liberation theology that were given to him as gifts). Romero publicly called him "brother" and "a great modern bishop." And he considered the version of liberation theology Pironio set forth to be providential. Christian liberation was, for Pironio, liberation from sin first of all. It went beyond the narrow horizons of history and socioeconomic levels. It was necessary to identify with the paschal mystery of Christ who came "to take away the sin of the world," with "the meaning of the redemptive incarnation," with "the beauty of the Gospel." Yet

Christian liberation was also justice. Romero wholeheartedly agreed with what Pironio said in 1971: "The Christian demand for justice is an integral part of the authentic preaching of the Gospel of peace. The religious message of the Church resides precisely in the total liberation of the person, which must not be identified with violence."

In October 1972 Romero told the clergy of San Salvador about a conference in Antigua, Guatemala, where the founder of liberation theology, the Peruvian priest Gustavo Gutiérrez, had given a talk. "Father Gutiérrez gave the impression of being a theologian who has matured a lot and who endeavors to explain in a balanced way a teaching that has so often been the object of exaggerated acceptance or rejection. He insists very much on pointing out the extremes into which one can fall, and continually underscores the balance of sound doctrine." A few weeks earlier, Paul VI had criticized a theological concept of "liberation" that did not respect evangelical liberty. He called it a "euphemism" that masked subversive methods and dangerous alliances with anti-Christian currents. For this reason they had listened to Gutiérrez with the Pope's observations in mind. Romero noted:

> We all joyfully noted that when the theology is explained in this way, it is not something else, as he himself said repeatedly. It is nothing other than the eternal theology of salvation, which cannot stop at the socio-political level and not even at a simple promotion of man. Instead, from the deepest level of Christian liberation from sin, it consistently radiates its human and social consequences.

As far as politics were concerned, in those years Romero shared the views of most of the Salvadoran bishops: Regardless of the degree of democracy, it was necessary to reach an agreement with the government in power so as to guarantee a place for the Church in society and also to collaborate for the good of the country. There was an alternative political option: to support the Christian Democrats. But CEDES did not back the Christian Democratic Party of Napoleón Duarte, which in the early seventies was also the most popular party and the one that received the most votes in El Salvador.

Beyond the noble phraseology of their pronouncements—talk about human rights and the denunciation of repressive abuses by the State—the Salvadoran bishops supported the stable military and oligarchical governments rather than the opposition composed of reform-minded Christian Democrats. If defeated, they would have dragged the Church down with them. Except for Chávez and Rivera, the Salvadoran bishops did not like the Christian Democrats. Instead they preferred to make high-level agreements with the government, over and above the political parties. The 1972 elections were marred by fraud and by the imprisonment, torture, and exile of Duarte. But CEDES took no clear position and had no words of sympathy for Duarte. In his public statements, Romero had a mandate to publicize the pronouncements of CEDES and dutifully kept to the evasive line of the bishops. On his own, however, he added an appeal to the civilians and the military. The President of the Republic had urged "civilians to see that Salvadorans in uniform are sons of El Salvador too." Romero endorsed the presidential appeal but considered it partial: The call to national brotherhood had to be a two-way street, "so that Salvadorans in uniform, who wield the power of weapons and enjoy the highest political positions, might consider well that defenseless civilians or those who have been defeated politically are brothers too. They are sons of the same fatherland and of the same God, and deserve the respect of their persons, their rights, and their legitimate aspirations."

Romero's sensitivity to human civil rights was not unconditional, for he also had to consider the stability of the country.

Nevertheless Romero sometimes would firmly oppose the government if he thought that justice required it. A certain penal law tried to allow extrajudicial confession by the accused. Consequently, statements obtained under torture would be taken as legitimate evidence in court. Romero observed that "a tremendous sense of discouragement and fear, not to mention terror, is spreading these days . . . knowing as we do what sort of methods the current 'justice' system employs to obtain such confessions." Romero opposed the section of the law that provided for two witnesses chosen by the judge to validate the extrajudicial confession:

> Who will be called as witnesses in the case of a delicate confession that has possible political implications? Will they be witnesses who will remain silent and be accomplices to the torture that they know about? Or will they be naive witnesses, who were not present at the torture just before the confession? And all this will remain with impunity in the hands of a judge according to whom the witnesses, surely chosen by him or by the security forces, are trustworthy?

These words were spoken by the Romero of 1973, not by the Romero in conflict with the government from 1977 to 1980.

Romero did not absolutize the value of democracy, but he willingly supported it in practice. When Paul VI spoke about democracy, Romero would repeat his words emphatically. After a visit to Costa Rica during the elections in 1973, Romero described with admiration the "democratic maturity" of that country, a brother to El Salvador, which succeeded in avoiding "electoral fraud." On the level of principles, Romero's political ideas were aligned with the magisterium. In particular, Romero was guided by referring to the social doctrine of the Church and to *Gaudium et Spes*. For Romero, both Marxism and capitalism were evils. Between 1970 and 1974, he made many negative pronouncements about Communism and [economic] liberalism, in rather rough language. He believed it was necessary to make changes to improve conditions in El Salvador but, as he sometimes quipped ironically, "the politicians who speak of change give the impression that they mean changing their shirt." He criticized the *caudillismo* of Salvadorans (that is, to treat leaders as if they were idols), and he considered it a sacred duty to go to the polls and vote.

Politically, Romero was guided by the most basic principle: the common good of the country. His was a twofold patriotism, national and Latin American, as is often the case in South and Central America. He didn't care for North Americans and their international politics, although he justified some aspects of it as necessary because of the Cold War. Romero was not a nationalist. His opinions of the brief war between Honduras and El Salvador in 1969 were not blindly patriotic, (whereas some bishops, on either side, had allowed themselves to be caught up in the militaristic furor). But his fatherland was an important value for him. Auxiliary Bishop Romero liked to speak about a radiant "Salvadoran destiny." He did not regard El Salvador mournfully as a victim, as if it were a small country that would always be marginalized and exploited. According to Romero, the universality of the Church saved nations from the narrowness of "immediate, local problems." In this sense, for Romero, Rome was his fatherland as much as El Salvador. When he was appointed bishop of Santiago de María in October 1974, he decided immediately to go to Rome. He felt that his new pastoral responsibility bound him even more closely to Rome in faith: "by a strange paradox of this same faith, the more my attachment to Rome grows, the more intimately I identify myself with my new diocese and my homeland."

The title of an article Romero wrote,"*Los campesinos no son parias,*" ["The Peasants Are Not Pariahs"] became a leitmotif in his statements. He denounced injustices, beatings, and outrages suffered by Salvadoran peasants at the hands of the landowners. The peasants were not pariahs but "citizens," besides being children of God. They had the right to form labor unions. The minimum wage had to be paid and necessities had to be reasonably priced. The peasants should not have to pay more for the consequences of economic crises and of bad harvests than the rich paid, although the latter routinely shifted the burden onto the people. ("The laborer is not a piece of merchandise, subject to the ups and downs of the economy, but a human person, and by that fact alone has the right to a just wage.")

Passing from principles to technical solutions to the rural problem, Romero had doubts about "structural reforms." His own proposal was not the traditional Catholic idea of forming a large class of landowning farmers who cultivated their own small pieces of land. Romero did not want to "leave behind the system of large estates so as to enter into a system of small estates"; the land of the country "would be atomized into four million whims and four million farmhouses in which four million egotists would hide." He called for a redistribution of land to favor a system of cooperatives. This would incentivize mutual solidarity and the modernization "of organization, planning, and technology." Similar ideas had met with the accusation of Communism, which he rebutted as follows:

> It has become commonplace to read daily accusations against the Church and her ministers on the pages of the daily press, in paid advertisements, or in opinion pieces by hack writers. They produce articles in series like sausages, with an ill-concealed anxiety to defend political or economic positions. A bishop intent on doing his pastoral duty can no longer speak without being branded as a Communist. A priest can no longer preach social justice without some people accusing him of extremist tendencies. Some Catholics do not even hesitate to make common cause with the enemies of the Church.

Romero also sternly called the attention of the ruling class to the issue of the family. The auxiliary bishop stressed the ruin of the Salvadoran family. Only 40 percent of children lived in what could be called an intact family, with both parents. And 73 percent of children under the age of five were malnourished. Eighty percent of Salvadorans lived in irregular unions, and 67 percent of the children were born outside of marriage and hence generally lacked "a father and [his] moral and material protection." According to Romero, the problems in Salvadoran families could not be isolated from those in society as a whole: unemployment, alcoholism, usury, eroticism, pornography, drugs, consumerism, and extravagant luxuries. Romero said the ruling class was primarily responsible for the social ills and disintegration of the family.

As an auxiliary bishop, Romero was a convinced supporter of papal pronouncements and of Vatican II. In his writings and homilies several of his favorite concepts reappear during his years as archbishop. The position he took regarding liberation theology during the early seventies remained essentially unchanged later on. The same can be said about his emphasis in the years 1970–1974 on patient dialogue in social and political conflicts, the urgent need for structural reform based on the conversion of hearts, the prophetic mission assigned to the Church (not on the same level as technical solutions to problems), and about the role of the priest, who should remain detached from politics while not neglecting the public forum. Romero's preaching from 1977–1980 contained many ideas that had already crystallized in the preceding years.

Romero had two non-negotiable priorities in his daily life: prayer and work. Once he had performed these duties, he spent his time with friends from various backgrounds. Some were at the seminary where he resided, among them Rogelio Esquivel and the aforementioned Rutilio Grande. Others were at the nunciature, including the

Australian councilor Edward Cassidy. Romero had friends in Opus Dei, and we should mention his confessor, Fernando Sáenz Lacalle, who was originally from Spain. Grande, Esquivel, Cassidy, and Sáenz were all clerics. Romero looked to them for "priestly integrity." Another sort of friendship, however, was especially dear to Romero. It was the friendship that he found among the simple people, with whom he could be his naturally affable self and establish familiar ties, as he did with Elvira Chacón and Salvador Barraza.

During Romero's years in San Miguel, he dropped in on the Chacón family at any time, asking for popular dishes like the fried beans that he loved so much and sipping big cups of coffee. Elvira Chacón, the very portrait of a housewife in an apron, with a big smile on her face, struggled together with her family to help Romero with the small necessities of daily life. Romero's departure from San Miguel would not weaken his bonds of affection for the Chacóns. He continued to visit them unexpectedly even when he was archbishop of San Salvador. When Romero was bishop of Santiago de María, Elvira went to prepare the meals for the conferences that he had with the priests or other guests.

Salvador Barazza was a cloth merchant in San Salvador. He had called on Romero in 1959, during a business trip to San Miguel, drawn by the fame of his preaching. Their friendship gradually grew closer. Barazza had taken care of moving Romero to San Salvador in 1967. In 1970 the Barazza family welcomed Romero into their home for three months while he was suffering from respiratory problems. Romero effectively became a member of their family.[5] He went to their house at unpredictable times and had his own space

---

5. Romero was godfather, or *compadre*, to the Barazzas' daughter Virginia, and therefore considered "co-parent" in the family. —*Ed.*

there: an armchair for a nap, the children who wanted to play with him, his place at the table, and a television to watch together. Joking often, at times Romero would also confide in the family. The youngest, Lupita (Guadalupe), would bring him his slippers and loosen his collar. Romero showed a unique kindness toward her, for Lupita had been born shortly before Romero came to San Salvador and had been gravely ill. Romero allowed her to call him Papa, Daddy, *papito*. With Salvador Barazza, Romero sometimes escaped to Mexico or Guatemala for short vacations, or just to go to the circus, of which he was a great fan.

To Santiago de María

On October 15, 1974, Romero was appointed bishop of Santiago de María, a small commercial center with a population of 12,000. It resembled many other quiet provincial towns of Central America. It had the added advantage of a high-altitude climate, which was much more pleasant than the torrid coast of El Salvador or the area around San Miguel. The diocese had almost a half-million faithful and about twenty parishes. Not every parish had a pastor because there were also only about twenty priests, some of them elderly. The diocese extended from the Pacific coast to the border of Honduras, from the ocean to the mountains, across the country. It reflected the social reality of rural El Salvador. The large coffee, cotton, and cane sugar plantations were owned by a few large landowners. Masses of peasants without land of their own worked for them seasonally (six months a year on average). Almost 70 percent of the population struggled with poverty.

Romero was returning to his origins. The diocese of Santiago had been formed in 1954, carved out of the diocese of San Miguel, where he had grown up. Its territory included Ciudad Barrios. Romero knew the clergy of Santiago well. It was made up of priests from San Miguel who had gone on to the new diocese.

At this point Romero no longer had immediate superiors. Now as he fulfilled his duties he was ultimately responsible for them. He no longer had to deal with secretariats, offices, newspapers, and institutional management. Instead he had a pastoral role, which he had not had in his previous seven years in San Salvador. The crucial question was no longer how to follow the official line or find the right balance, but how to provide pastoral care (*cura animarum*). Romero did not change in his faith, spirituality, or asceticism. Rather a new pastoral orientation was required of him. In the two years that he spent in Santiago before being sent to San Salvador as archbishop, Romero developed the ability to perform his episcopal ministry with impassioned pastoral sensitivity.

Recalling an address Pironio had given to his faithful Argentines of Mar del Plata, Romero described his ideal of a bishop in these terms in January 1976:

> A bishop can communicate the things of God and interpret history and human problems only in terms of the depth of faith. To be a sociologist, economist, or political scientist is neither his competence nor his task. He is simply a man of God in the service of all his brothers and sisters. . . . A bishop is not a technician, an administrator, or a boss. A bishop is essentially a pastor, a father, a brother, and a friend. He journeys with other people, sows hope along their path, shares their sorrow and joy, urges them to seek peace, in justice and love, and teaches them to be brothers and sisters. . . .

During his two years in Santiago, Romero gradually was able to connect with most of the faithful, win the confidence of the priests, and interest everyone with his gifts as a preacher. He displayed tremendous, albeit disorderly, dynamism. This led him to travel continuously through the streets, the cantons, the villages, and the most remote corners of the diocese, with its far-flung, understaffed ecclesiastical structures. (Some parishes had 50,000 parishioners and others had no pastor.) He had equipped a jeep with loudspeakers. Very often he could be seen setting out for the countryside early in the morning when the peasants were going to work. The pastors were seldom informed about these missions "on the go." (After all, they had difficulties adequately serving their vast parishes.) He preached from the jeep in the open air, stopped to talk with people, administered the sacraments, and distributed aid.

Romero strove to be a good bishop in the classic Tridentine manner. He developed good relations with the clergy, showed concern for the seminarians, visited the sick and the imprisoned, and provided for the liturgical decorum of the churches. Yet he also encouraged lay associations, such as the Cursillo Movement or Alcoholics Anonymous. He started clubs for the poor in Santiago and Usulután, the principal city of the diocese. In the parishes he set up Caritas committees, a result of Vatican II, anticipating their spread in the other dioceses of El Salvador. He enthusiastically promoted base communities after Paul VI mentioned them in *Evangelii Nuntiandi*.[6]

Romero arrived in Santiago assailed by doubts about his ability to befriend the clergy and promote the unity of the presbyterate. He tried to have personal conversations with everyone, especially the priests. This was a novelty compared to the style of his predecessor,

---

6. Base communities are small groups within the local churches that come together for particular purposes of spirituality or mission. They can vary quite a bit from place to place. —*Ed.*

Castro y Ramírez. Although a great orator, he was an administrator who rarely received visitors or went outside the chancery. Romero organized times spent with the clergy, such as spiritual exercises, family-style meals, and mornings on the majestic ocean beaches. He thought that he had to humble himself in order to be loved by his priests and his faithful. He asked for their help. He made an effort to show affection, to remember all his co-workers and their concerns, even their material needs. During a retreat with the diocesan clergy he asked them to critique him, and they told him his faults publicly. On various occasions he asked forgiveness of priests whom he had treated impulsively a little earlier.

Romero was more serene in Santiago than in San Salvador. Constantly with the people, he traveled along the road preaching and conversing. Where there were no roads for the jeep, he reached the villages by riding a horse or a mule. He liked to be close to the poor. He had no personal problems: the work was urgent and he had few doubts about what he had to do. Romero freely expressed his soul, which was dedicated to pastoral care of the people. As he had done in the past in San Miguel, he communicated with the people, was well liked, and succeeded in uniting the clergy around himself. He had a great desire to work. Being used to sleeping only a few hours each night, he further reduced the time he spent resting, saying that a little deep sleep was enough.

Although Romero knew well the humble circumstances of his people, he was still moved by the social situation in the diocese. He used to visit huts made of cane and mud or raw bricks, with an earthen floor and a sheet-metal roof that grew hot in the tropical sun. Seeing the poverty, sickness, unemployment, alcoholism, and illiteracy, he increased the number of charitable projects sponsored by the diocese. During the seasons of intense agricultural work, laborers thronged into the hilly city of Santiago. Some came from

distant villages. Masses of them slept in the public squares in the
cold nights of harvest season. Romero opened the diocesan buildings to offer them shelter. Then he had soup kitchens organized to
provide hot meals in the evening. Sometimes he dined with the
workers and listened as they told their life stories.

Romero knew that some landowners, sometimes the same ones
who supported the Church, broke the laws about the minimum
wage for rural workers. He began to voice requests for justice in
regard to their economic treatment. One of his articles about the
coffee harvesters concluded with strong words by the apostle after
whom the diocese was named:

> God, always glorious in his works, is giving us also in this year that
> splendid rain of rubies [i.e., ripe coffee beans] that draws thou-
> sands of hands from everywhere to gather the rich gift of our
> mountains. . . . The joy of the harvest gladdens us. It is not only
> the joy of the landowners but also the full happiness of so many
> harvesters, who with this harvest hope to obtain their income for
> the whole year. Yet it also saddens and concerns us to see the self-
> ishness with which methods and arrangements are found to limit
> the just wage of the harvesters. Think for example of this new
> category of helpers used to designate those who really are harvest-
> ers so as to deprive them of their legitimate pay. How we wish that
> the joy of this rain of rubies and of all the harvests of the earth
> would not be darkened by the tragic sentence of the Bible:
> "Behold, the wages of the laborers who mowed your fields, which
> you kept back by fraud, cry out; and the cries of the harvesters
> have reached the ears of the Lord of hosts" (James 5:4).

In June 1975, in the hamlet of Tres Calles near the coast, five
civilians were murdered by a detachment of the National Guard
who were conducting a surprise nighttime operation to terrorize
the peasants of that area, where agrarian conflicts often flared. The
incident made a lasting impression on Romero, who traveled there

and was moved to see the sorrow of the widows and orphans. He decided to write a long letter of vehement protest to President Molina. Romero described the torment of the victims' family members and of the "dear faithful of the canton of Tres Calles" and their feelings of "terror and indignation." He reminded the populace of the "Christian principle that violence only causes violence and evil." Nevertheless, a "just punishment" was necessary for those who transgressed God's laws, especially "the commandment not to kill." It was unacceptable to excuse the killings by claiming that the victims had committed crimes, because it was completely unlawful for a "security force" to claim the right to kill instead of arresting the guilty so as to bring them to trial. Romero had thought that the President of the Republic was his friend. They had met several times, and Molina had even boasted that "Romero was his spiritual father." But Romero's protest had no effect. The government did not investigate the incident at Tres Calles but shelved it instead.

Soon Romero had another reason for conflict with the civil authorities. A Spanish Passionist priest, Juan Macho Merino, was turned back at the airport in San Salvador. He was compelled to return to Spain on the same plane he had just flown on, with Iberia Airlines, although his documents were in order. Padre Macho was one of the organizers of the Lor Naranjos training center for rural catechists in the diocese of Santiago. The center gave both religious and sociopolitical classes based on an interpretation that would have then been called "Medellinist," that is, inspired by the Conference of Latin American Bishops in Medellín, Colombia. They had attempted to implement the Second Vatican Council for Latin America. The conference had been held in the revolutionary atmosphere of 1968, and many of the bishops were unaware that its theology had yielded somewhat to the social and political sciences.

One of the most influential ideas from the documents of Medellín was the call for the Church's involvement in the liberation of peoples from oligarchic political systems and from capitalist economic systems.

Romero was unsure of what to do about Los Naranjos, whether he should approve of its activities or disband it. He was worried because the catechetical center "placed great emphasis on sociology and politics," as he put it when writing to the Sacred Congregation for the Clergy in Rome asking for advice. Furthermore he was being pressured by landowners and civil authorities who opposed Los Naranjos. Nevertheless the outrage committed by the police at Father Macho's expense prompted him to defend his priest without hesitation, denying that he had any accusation or misgiving whatsoever in his regard. Romero wrote again to Molina, informing him that the Passionist priest enjoyed his "confidence as to his ideology and priestly conduct" and was a "true follower of the Gospel of Our Lord." If the President had "some just complaint" against Macho, Romero would be grateful to learn about it; otherwise it would be good to reconsider the case and to allow the priest to reenter the country. Molina acceded to Romero's request, and a few weeks later the Passionist was able to reenter El Salvador. Romero did not intend to allow the civil authorities to judge the work of a priest who had violated no law of the State. Later on, Romero promoted Father Macho to his pastoral vicar and encouraged Los Naranjos to continue its activities.

Orlando Cabrera, a frequent visitor and friend of Romero from the time he was a pastor in Ciudad Barrios in the sixties, saw Bishop Romero of Santiago as "a dreamer." No doubt Romero dreamed of great pastoral developments that would enliven and build up the diocese, which had been founded recently. It was structurally weak, and he knew that most of the people had been evangelized only superficially. For this reason, too, Romero did not want to get bogged down in conflicts and internal disputes. He was not interested in dividing his co-workers and the movements in the Church into good and bad, orthodox and heterodox. He accepted and encouraged them all: Opus Dei and "liberationists," "sacramentalist" priests and social-justice priests, old and young, conservatives and innovators, provided that they contributed to the *cura animarum*, the pastoral care of souls. Recognizing different charisms, synthesizing ideas and ways of implementing them, and most importantly promoting unity, were part of his job as bishop.

In Santiago, Romero was not transformed into a different man but was living in a new situation, an intense pastoral experience. He felt greater responsibility toward the poor, who were not strangers to him. His mental horizons broadened. He asked himself more urgent questions about social justice. This happened as a continuous development of his character, interior life, and emotions. When he left Santiago for San Salvador, Romero knew what it meant to be a bishop, to have responsibility for a people, to guide a presbyterate. He had succeeded in making himself well-liked by the clergy. He understood that a bishop governs a pluralistic reality. In his letter inviting the clergy of Santiago to attend his installation ceremony in San Salvador, written the day before he assumed his new office, Romero wrote about "two years" marked by "extremely rich priestly experiences, by which we helped one another to mature."

Primate of a Nation in Crisis

On February 3, 1977, Romero was nominated to be the archbishop of San Salvador and thus the Catholic primate of the country.[7] The history of El Salvador was entering a turbulent, tragic phase. A three-year passion awaited Romero, and finally, martyrdom. What was happening?

In the late seventies, the small country of El Salvador, whose reputation had never gone beyond the regional Central American context, was thrust into the world's attention. In its polarized society, an oligarchy that was insensitive to human rights confronted political currents that urgently demanded social justice. There was a military government, a highly privileged elite, many poor people, an emerging guerrilla movement, and circles that dreamed about Castro-style revolution. These factors were common to other countries in Latin America, yet El Salvador was a separate case.

The internal cause of the crisis was unusual, for it did not result from underdevelopment but from growth. Beginning in 1960, El Salvador had good economic indicators. The gross national product (GNP) of El Salvador had increased at an average annual rate of 5.5 percent in the sixties, and of 6.4 percent in the seventies. It fell in 1979 (-1.2 percent) because of the internal political crisis. A little prosperity was enough to upset longstanding balances. In the nineteenth century, Alexis de Tocqueville had this insight: the availability of more resources makes injustice less tolerable and provokes major crises.

But an external cause was also at work. The tiny country on the isthmus was becoming a crucial spot in the Cold War, which had reignited at the end of the seventies. (This was due to such things as

---

7. The primate held a certain position of leadership with regard to the other bishops of a country. Present canon law does not give any specific authority to the primate.

the Vietnamese occupation of Cambodia, the Iran crisis, Castro's sympathizers in Grenada, the Sandinista victory in Nicaragua, the Soviet invasion of Afghanistan, and renewed worldwide competition between the United States and the U.S.S.R.). In El Salvador the United States was preparing to draw the line of resistance against their Communist adversary in the Americas. A lot of blood would flow beginning in 1977. People disappeared, the lives of the peasants no longer had value, the guerrillas kidnapped and killed in retaliation, and the civil war that would break out in 1980 had begun to brew.

In 1977 El Salvador had four million inhabitants on almost 21,040 square kilometers [8,124 square miles]. Because of its prolonged economic growth, few predicted its slide into civil war. For decades, the oligarchy had held political power through the military, thus preventing democratic political developments. But the rulers had modernized the country. El Salvador no longer grew only coffee. Other crops suitable for export had been planted (cotton and sugar cane), industrial activity had been launched, and a good infrastructure had been put in place. The Salvadoran oligarchy was made up of families of Iberian but also of British, German, Dutch, and Jewish origin. They were more enterprising than other Latin American ruling classes and reinvested their profits, preferably locally. They did so out of pride, considering the country as their property. In other words, the oligarchs identified the nation, the State—all of El Salvador—with themselves. To them it was incomprehensible that others should aspire to govern the country that they had created, built, and educated. They viewed their opponents as enemies of the fatherland, as an anti-nation.

The economic growth had been inequitable. It was often said that fourteen families of the oligarchy controlled the entire Salvadoran economy. The country's ruling class was actually larger, but it is true that the huge profits from exported cash crops ended up in a few hands. In 1980, 20 percent of the population produced 66 percent of the GNP, and the poorest 20 percent produced only 2 percent. The rural masses were impoverished. Hunger was felt in many places and in many seasons. The lands left for producing food-stuffs to support the peasant families had gradually been reduced by the greed of the landowners who extended the acreage dedicated to export crops. The rural population had decreased to 52 percent in 1980, whereas it had been 68 percent in 1950.

The cities did not experience the same hardship as the country-side due to urban development. The statistics on education showed progress: literacy had increased from 38 percent of the population in 1950 to 60 percent in 1975, and the number of university students had tripled between 1961 and 1979. These factors of greater urbanization, more access to schools, the birth of a middle class, and wider newspaper circulation—in short, a modern culture—urgently required transforming the country. Since 1932 it had been governed uninterruptedly by the military, to which the oligarchy had delegated the task of keeping order in the country while they dedicated themselves to business.

The cities had some growth of democratic rule through the political parties. Nevertheless, both in 1972 and in 1977 the election results had been manipulated. Two military officers, first Colonel Arturo Armando Molina and then General Carlos Humberto Romero, had become president. Although Napoleón Duarte and Ernesto Claramount were the actual winners of the two elections, with center-left coalitions, they both had been forced into exile and considered themselves lucky that their lives had been spared. In theory, El Salvador was a democratic country, with political pluralism, a parliamentary system, and a constitutional order. In practice, a restricted elite jealously wielded power. The forms of lawful democracy were respected, but the regime was essentially authoritarian. It prevented opposing political groups from expressing their views, and it stifled the beginnings of social movements, starting with labor unions. In reaction, an armed opposition had gradually formed in the country beginning from 1970.

When Romero became archbishop of San Salvador, he immediately had to deal with all this: the military in power and the oligarchy that backed them, a legal but humiliated and marginalized opposition party, and the energetic political activism of the so-called popular organizations, which were fascinated by an armed solution. The latter included extra-parliamentary political groups, rural labor unions, and revolutionary student groups. Even more, the leaders of the popular organizations had mutual ties with the guerrilla groups. The popular organizations had transparent structures and well-known programs. But their public political activities coexisted with the clandestine activity of the underground politico-military organizations. This collaboration was kept secret for reasons of expediency. This dualist revolutionary system was peculiar to El Salvador in those years, although it drew its inspiration from reformed Guevarism, which held that, "neither weapons without the people, nor the people without weapons" could produce a victorious revolution.

During Romero's years as archbishop, the descent into war and the national tragedy could be foreseen. Violent conflict was in the air. On one side stood the arrogance of the military government and of the restricted ruling class; on the other stood the stubborn determination to challenge the prevailing order. Civil war was not a fatal destiny for El Salvador. In the positive economic climate of the late sixties, the Christian Democratic Party had emerged as a force capable of winning elections and governing. But the oligarchy and the military, fearful of Christian Democratic reform, did not want to give up their power. As mentioned earlier, Duarte won the election in 1972. But the opposing candidates then stole the election and violently repressed protests. The incident made it clear that it would be impossible to bring about political change by democratic means. The political battle became more radical. The rise of guerrilla groups and popular organizations siding with the opposition was countered by repressive paramilitary units and then by death squads. The violent repression fueled the nascent guerrilla warfare, which gained sympathizers among the victims of the military forces' brutality. *Unión Guerriera Blanca* [White Warring Union] was the cruelest group of extreme right assassins. The most-feared private militia was ORDEN [*Organización Democrática Nacionalista*, or Democratic Nationalist Organization]. It supported the landowners' interests in the countryside.

The level of brutality varied with the occasions and the surroundings. The violence of the right was characterized by displays of cruelty. It was no accident that the victims were mutilated and disfigured in horrifying ways to instill terror. The violence of the left included killings, kidnappings, and crimes. This was more deliberately targeted to finance its own operations, to acquire weapons, and to radicalize the people by stirring up unrest through clashes in public squares.

El Salvador differed from neighboring countries on the isthmus and from other Latin American countries because of the widespread presence of Catholics in the popular movements and guerrilla groups. They were even a dominant presence in the lower levels, though less so in the leadership. Many guerrilla fighters came from social Catholicism, from the rural Catholic labor unions, from the Christian Democratic Party, from base communities, or from parishes and lay Catholic associations affected by the ideas of liberation theology. The Catholics in the popular organizations and in the guerrilla military groups absorbed Marxist teaching and vocabulary. But in turn they influenced the culture of the militant Marxists, who were weak because of their division into mutually antagonistic groups. The number of Communists in El Salvador was not large enough to enable them to easily integrate the mass of militant Catholics, who made up most of the opposition to the regime. If they lost their faith, it happened less because of their conversion to Marxism than because they gave absolute priority to their earthly endeavors. What remained, however, as a mark of their origin was their exaltation of suffering, sacrifice, martyrdom, and salvific death, in keeping with the standard of the cross and resurrection.

In El Salvador the Catholic Church had had good relations with the ruling classes. As elsewhere in Latin America, the oligarchy had supported Catholicism, financed the clergy, and donated money to build churches. Catholicism, in exchange, had supported the established order and had guaranteed the stability of the regimes. The Salvadoran ruling classes reacted violently to the Catholic interest in social issues. The oligarchy was furious most of all about the labor unions organized among the peasants, for this directly affected its economic interests. The rulers felt betrayed by the Catholic Church, which until then had built its churches and paid its clergy's salaries with money from the oligarchy. Now the Church was rebelling against them. Yet many oligarchs were not practicing Catholics, although they had built churches. They had financed the religion as a pillar of their social order. Now the clergy ceased to be economically supported by the Salvadoran oligarchy. Its autonomy was seen as an about-face. Hence hatred grew not only for individual priests singled out as subversives and Communists, but also for the Church as a whole.

Suddenly, Catholics were no longer reliable. Better to trust the Protestants. Indeed, the seventies saw North American neo-Protestant Pentecostals begin to invade El Salvador—not unlike the situation in other Latin American countries with similar domestic crises. In the Salvadoran countryside during Romero's years as archbishop, the mere fact of having a Bible in one's house could result in death if the family was Catholic. That did not happen if the family was Protestant. The oligarchy transferred the confidence that it had lost in the Catholics to the Protestants, as though the whole Church had become Communist and subversive. In the late seventies, the Salvadoran media constantly attacked the Church. Between December 1976 and May 1977, when Romero settled in the capital, the four main daily newspapers in El Salvador ran sixty-two paid advertisements against the Church. These were placed by landowners' associations or fictitious groups. In those same months those newspapers ran thirty-two editorials against the Church. Salvadoran Catholics defended themselves by publishing, at their own cost, twenty-three press releases, but they obtained only a few favorable editorials. One slogan of the extreme right was plastered on walls all over the country: *"Haga patria, mate a un cura"* ("Be patriotic, kill a priest"). In *La Cartilla del Soldado*, the basic textbook for training recruits, the Catholic Church was treated as a force "allied with Communism." Priests were described as "elements dangerous to national security." So began a persecution against the Church and against Catholics in El Salvador.

Chapter Three

Archbishop of San Salvador

First Days and the Death of Rutilio Grande

 In December 1976 tensions increased between the Salvadoran government and the Catholic Church, which was accused of undermining the public order. The Jesuits in El Salvador faced the threat of expulsion. Archbishop Chávez had always kept up relations with the government, either good or not so good. But in December 1976, President Molina refused his phone calls. The prelate continued to maintain that social injustice was at the root of the widespread violence in the nation. Tired and disillusioned, Chávez decided to resign shortly before the end of his lengthy mandate, which had begun in 1938.

The Holy See had already named his successor: Romero. Rome had a largely positive file on him, since he had been a favorite of the last few nuncios in El Salvador.

Romero's transfer from Santiago de María to the capital was not the result of any pressuring on his part. If he could have chosen where to be bishop, Romero would have preferred to go to San Miguel, "his" city. Romero was flattered by Rome's trust. He nonetheless doubted his own abilities in a difficult situation like the one the archdiocese faced, all the more so in a time of intense conflict between State and Church.

He had little time to prepare. He officially assumed the new office on February 22, 1977. Just one day earlier, the government had harassed several foreign priests accused of political subversion and expelled them from El Salvador. A pastor was seriously injured in the diocese of San Vicente. Newspaper, radio, and television media were almost completely in the hands of the ruling class. For weeks they had been running an intimidation campaign against the Catholic Church, which they accused of engaging in politics and of fomenting the peasant uprising against the established order. In early December 1976, Eduardo Orellana, a plantation owner in the area of Aguilares, about twenty kilometers north of the capital, was shot to death in an altercation with members of a peasant union with Christian roots. The police made no arrests, but the Salvadoran media blamed the death on the clergy, who—they claimed—were promoting rural unionization. They called for the application of an article of the Salvadoran Constitution that prohibited the use of "religious motives" or "religious beliefs" for the purpose of "engaging in political propaganda." It also prohibited criticism in churches of the laws and of the national government.

On that same day, February 22, 1977, Romero and the other Salvadoran bishops went to visit Molina. He had lost the election but would remain in office for several more months, until the transition of power on July 1, 1977. Molina did not waste a moment lamenting his electoral defeat or congratulating Romero as the new archbishop. Instead he bitterly told the bishops that the Church had strayed from the right path and needed to be brought back to it. The Salvadoran associations of landowners were convinced that the Church, and particularly Chávez and the Jesuits, were to blame for the labor unions formed among the rural workers. But was it wrong? Unions were an accepted reality throughout the civilized world. Rather, the labor market in El Salvador was outdated in opposing unions. In a meeting of the bishops' conference (CEDES), Rivera Damas maintained that "it was necessary to reject the idea that the just wage preached by the Church is a Communist precept, and to make very clear that it is a Christian precept."

Romero did not present himself to the archdiocese as a returning victor after the disputes he had had with clergy in the early seventies. Neither did he proceed to make any public presentation or to take office officially. The nation faced a time of deep crisis. Presidential elections had been held on February 20. Molina was no longer the candidate of the strong Salvadoran forces, for it was thought that he hadn't sufficiently defended the oligarchy's interests. The candidate was a general with the surname Romero, but who was not related to the archbishop. Carlos Humberto Romero had won through fraud. His opponent, Colonel Ernesto Claramount of the military, had denounced the deception, and his supporters had taken to the public squares. A state of siege had been proclaimed in the country.

Carlos Romero, having taken office in those hours, did not have a handle on the situation. The repression of public protests began during the night of February 27. A massacre occurred. On February 28 an assembly of urban clergy nominated three diocesan priests to deal with the political and humanitarian emergency and to draft reports for the new archbishop. Romero appreciated the initiative. On March 5, CEDES issued a statement protesting the violence erupting throughout the country against the peasants, clergy, and ordinary citizens, pointing out that it originated in the social injustices affecting most of the population. Romero had helped draft the declaration, which spoke in no uncertain terms. On March 10, Romero appeared at an assembly of diocesan clergy on the emergency situation facing the Church. He was able to listen in person to many accounts of harassment and threats. While Romero was getting his bearings in the archdiocese and learning about what was happening in the country, a fateful day arrived—March 12, 1977. On that day, Rutilio Grande and two peasants who were with him, an elderly man and a young boy, were killed on the road to Aguilares. The murder was intended as revenge for the death of Eduardo Orellana in the same area three months earlier. The incident shocked Romero, who was a close friend of Grande's.

Rutilio Grande was a sensitive, generous, restless man. He was one of the Jesuits of El Salvador. They presented themselves as a solid and unified body, but subtle differences existed among them. Rutilio was Salvadoran, not of Spanish descent like many of his confreres. He did not share the passion for politics that was common among the Jesuit scholars at Central American University, whom he facetiously called "the teachers of Israel." He humbly disagreed with Father Ignacio Ellacuría,[1] the outstanding intellectual of the Jesuits in El Salvador. At the UCA Ellacuría had theoretically discussed

---

1. Government forces killed Father Ignacio Ellacuría with five other Jesuits and two employees on November 16, 1989. —*Ed.*

political change of the country through reform. Born near Bilbao, Ellacuría was European and believed in the power of reason to impose the truth. Rutilio, on the other hand, believed in passion and love inspired by the Gospel. Ellacuría adopted, in essence, an old and effective recipe of the Jesuit apostolate, applying it to religious as well as temporal matters. By imparting high culture, the UCA aimed to create an alternative ruling class that would revolutionize the country.

Rutilio loved those whom he called "the massive oppressed majorities" of the Salvadoran people. He distinguished them from the wealthy urban minorities whom he gladly left to the care of his confreres at the UCA. He had declined an academic post so that he could live among the peasants. He believed that the only solution to the troubles of El Salvador, with its rural soul, was to communicate the Gospel to the peasants. Rutilio preached love for and among the peasants; he was not interested in speaking to the rich. He lived austerely in a little room marked by monastic simplicity: a bed, a night stand, a small candle, and a Bible. Over four years he created a movement of Christian communities in the parish of Aguilares, in which two thousand *campesinos* [peasant farmers] participated.

Rutilio did not wish to become involved in political plans and strategies. One of his confreres wrote this: "He had the conviction that following Jesus and his Gospel could bring about a more profound change in people and institutions than any political program." Nevertheless, Rutilio saw how his actions provoked agitation in political groups and unions. He did not oppose the actions of peasants who demanded better wages in the name of Christian justice and who banded together to achieve this. But he was a peaceful man who did not want social change to be brought about through violence. For Rutilio, conversion was devoting himself to pastoral care and loving the peasants, just as for Ellacuría, conversion was fighting for the truth. That translated into the urgent need for change in the country's politics with a view to social justice that would bring the kingdom of God closer to earth. In a fraternal spirit, Rutilio's mission in Aguilares competed with the UCA for the young Jesuits who needed to receive new assignments. Many preferred Aguilares to the capital.

Romero considered Rutilio a man of God. While hesitant in his close friendships with other priests, Romero had always trusted Rutilio, a genuine friend. Romero reached the small church in Aguilares a few hours after the murder of his friend and the two peasants. It was evening. Deeply moved, Romero spent the night in prayerful vigil over the bodies of the three victims. Romero and the peasants filled the little church. Romero felt that they had been left orphans by their "father" and that it was up to him, as archbishop and Rutilio's close friend, to take his place in some way. He also reflected on God's will for his new ministry, marked from the beginning by the blood of a person so dear to him and so precious to his local Church. In the homily at the funeral the day after the murder, Romero preached with great emotion: "In truly important times of my life, he was very close to me, and such gestures are never forgotten." Taking inspiration from *Evangelii Nuntiandi*, Romero spoke of the liberation offered by the Church, which his murdered friend had believed in:

> The liberation that Grande preached is inspired by the faith. A faith that speaks to us about eternal life, a faith that he now, with his face lifted up to heaven and accompanied by two farmers, offers in its entirety, in its perfection. Liberation that ends in happiness in God, liberation that starts with repentance for sin, liberation that is based on Christ, the only saving strength: this is the liberation that Rutilio Grande preached. . . . If only the movements that are sensitive to the social question had known it. . . .

Unless a conversion is experienced in the heart . . . everything will be feeble, revolutionary, transient, violent. Not Christian.

Romero emphasized in particular the "motivation of love" that had guided Rutilio:

True love is what drew Rutilio Grande to his death, along with two peasants. That is how he loved the Church: he died with them, and with them he appeared as he moved on to heaven. He loved them. It is significant that Father Grande was shot just as he was traveling to his people to bring them the message of the Mass and of salvation. A priest with his peasants, going to his people to identify with them, to live with them: not a revolutionary inspiration, but an inspiration of love and precisely because love is what inspires us, as brothers and sisters. . . .

The death of Rutilio Grande shook Romero and caused him to question his mission. It also had crucial repercussions on Romero's course of action. It led him to confront President Molina, the government, and the oligarchy head-on. This damaged relations with the papal nuncio, Emanuele Gerada, who a few weeks earlier had worked to have him named archbishop. It created a powerful unity between Romero and diocesan clergy, which the new archbishop could not have hoped for just a few days earlier. All of this happened in just one week.

The Clash with the Government

On March 12, merely a few hours after the murder of Rutilio Grande, President Molina phoned Romero. He told him the sad news and promised to provide him immediately with an official report on the incident. Romero thanked him for his condolences. On March 14, he wrote to Molina saying that he would not participate in any official function of the government until it had shed full light on the sacrilegious murder of Grande. Molina responded that day. He reiterated that he had ordered a thorough investigation and suggested that the crime was a provocation meant to disrupt the nation's peace. Within a few days Romero realized that the criminal investigation was not being conducted with the intention of shedding light on it. Romero was certain that Molina wanted to cover the tracks of those responsible and reinterpreted the phone call on March 12 as an act of "cynicism."

Romero met with Molina on March 23 and presented him with several requests: to explain the circumstances of Rutilio Grande's murder; to guarantee the freedom and safety of the many threatened priests and catechists; to allow deported priests to reenter the country; and to stop violent organizations like the Democratic Nationalist Organization (*Organización Democrática Nacionalista*, ORDEN). One especially important point for Romero concerned the priests whom the government thought were involved in politics. The archbishop asked that neither the civil authorities nor the security forces act unilaterally in their regard. Romero wanted their cases to be discussed with church authorities, guaranteeing that he himself would work to prevent abuses and violations of the law. Molina proved his good will by granting the archbishop's requests. But he said that international Communism had wanted Grande killed, and El Salvador's judicial system could not ensure a successful outcome of the ongoing investigations. Romero deduced from this that those responsible for the death of Rutilio Grande would not be brought to justice.

Before Molina left office on July 1, Romero had other contacts and meetings with him, either individually or with the other bishops of the country. The tone grew more unpleasant each time. Molina presumed to determine which priests were "good" and which were "bad." He accused the Church of meddling in politics and of inciting the peasants against the authorities.

In their discussions, Molina had always agreed that the individual cases of priests whom the government suspected of being subversive would be addressed beforehand by the civil authorities together with the bishops. But in reality this promise was not always kept, especially in 1977. Romero's notes on his meetings with Molina repeatedly contain phrases like: "remind him of the agreement to dialogue with the bishop before intervening about any priest." Molina did nothing to soften the public attitudes that incited a lynch-mob atmosphere in regard to the Church, the clergy, and Christians involved in social action. A personal conflict developed between Romero and Molina, for reasons of justice and dignity. Romero felt offended by the nation's president both because he seemed to be protecting the murderers of Rutilio Grande, and because he would publicly repeat what Romero discussed with him, despite their confidentiality agreement. Romero insisted that the government handle privately, with the church authorities, any problems with priests accused of political activism. Molina used this request to declare publicly that not only were some clergymen subversive, but also that the bishops knew it.

Another of Romero's priests, Alfonso Navarro, was killed on May 11, as was a boy who was with him in the rectory in the center of San Salvador. The previous day the body of Mauricio Borgonovo Pohl had been found. He was the Minister of Foreign Affairs and belonged to one of the most powerful families of the oligarchy. Borgonovo had been kidnapped by a guerrilla group and murdered after the government had decided not to negotiate for his release. A far-right terrorist organization chose to symbolically avenge Borgonovo's death by killing a priest. They erroneously thought Navarro was a member of the detested Society of Jesus. When shortly after Navarro's murder Romero received a phone call from Molina offering his condolences, it seemed to Romero that he was experiencing a cynical *déjà vu*.

On May 17 a large contingent of troops moved toward Aguilares, where three Jesuits in Rutilio Grande's group were still working. Peasants had been occupying land there. Two thousand soldiers surrounded the town of Aguilares and searched the homes one by one in order to intimidate the people. Many civilians were killed: six according to the government; around a hundred according to other sources. The three Jesuits were arrested, beaten, and expelled from the country. In the little church in Aguilares, the soldiers opened the tabernacle, scattered the consecrated hosts on the floor, and trampled on them. Romero rushed there but was prevented from entering the town. Turned back by the soldiers, he sent the military chaplain of the National Guard, whom the soldiers took into custody. On May 23 Romero wrote an indignant letter to Molina about the events in Aguilares: "I do not understand, Mr. President, how on the one hand you declare to the nation that you are a Catholic by education and conviction, and on the other hand you allow these undeniable abuses by security forces in a country we call civilized and Christian."

The Aguilares case would come to exemplify the strategy of repressing peasant unrest and Catholic social action. Eduardo Orellana was killed there, and for the families of the oligarchy he had risen to the status of a martyr. The hated Jesuits worked there. The social conflict was more acute there than in most other parts of the country due to the extensive sugar cane plantations, which led to vast underemployment among manual laborers. From 1977 on, the area of Aguilares would be subjected to continual repression, much more than other districts. The Christian communities founded by Rutilio Grande were scattered. Nearly all of the roughly four hundred catechists in the Aguilares region were physically eliminated, year after year.

The Aguilares incident definitively convinced Romero of the reality of a persecution of the Church and a barbarism that afflicted the population. Meanwhile, acts of terrorism began, damaging archdiocesan buildings. In the spring of 1977, the archdiocesan printing offices were bombed. It then became customary to use dynamite against the Catholic institutions of San Salvador.

Romero would have gladly avoided confrontation with the government. But he felt compelled by the crimes that he saw being committed, and by the disappearances, murders, and torture that he learned about. He didn't want a conflict with the government because he was a man of order who respected the law and established agreements. In his heart, he hoped that the government officials would reform their ways. "Our purpose is not a conflict with the civil authorities," he declared to Cardinal Baggio in December 1977. He added: "We constantly have distressing cases that worry us a lot. But we continue working and hoping that, through concrete efforts, the climate of trust necessary for truly constructive dialogue will be restored."

If the Church were attacked, however, Romero responded. On May 8, 1977, he cited Pius XI from the pulpit: "When politics touches the altar, the Church defends the altar." The previous April, while visiting Rome, Romero had gone to pray at the tomb of Pius XI. He recalled the following words, which the pope had taken as his inspiration in combating the various forms of totalitarianism: "As long as I live, no one will laugh at the Church." As Romero wrote to Baggio in May 1978, he felt it was his duty to imitate the "holy bishop of Milan, Ambrose, when he prohibited the Emperor Theodosius from entering the church, requiring him to first do public penance for his sin of unjustly massacring civilians." The dramatic comparison revealed a strong sense of the Church's mission and of the bishop's responsibility in dealing with abuses of political power. Romero continued:

> I thought it was my duty not to attend the inauguration of the new President of the Republic [General Romero]. His responsibility in the tragic events just mentioned is undeniable, since during almost the entire previous Presidency he held the office of Minister of Defense and National Security, and afterward was elected President himself. Nevertheless I showed that I was open to dialogue with the President. I declared this repeatedly from my throne in the cathedral, highlighting in various homilies whatever good I was able to find in his inauguration speech. For all that—so as not to be manipulated into conferring religious legitimacy on a government that until now has been so distant from the common good—I thought it my duty to make this dialogue conditional on deeds, not just on apparently well-meaning words. I indicated fair conditions for the desired dialogue with the President: ending the repression and harassment of the peasants and their legitimate organizations, making an effort to shed light on the disappearances of many citizens, and reconsidering the expulsions of exiled priests.

After Rutilio Grande's murder, the deaths of Borgonovo and Navarro were another dramatic episode in the new archbishop's relations with the Salvadoran ruling class. Romero had worked privately and publicly, offering his services as a mediator for the liberation of Minister Borgonovo. His abduction lasted several weeks before its tragic conclusion, which had an emotional impact on public opinion. Romero then celebrated the funeral of the unfortunate Minister of Foreign Affairs, spoke Christian words of comfort and compassion for a man he knew as peaceful and open to dialogue, and consoled the family members. He had been in contact with them for weeks. A little later, Romero celebrated the funeral of

Father Navarro. Romero's funeral homily for Borgonovo had a mournful tone, but the homily for his priest was fervent and heart-rending. This was understandable because Romero, as the bishop, felt a special sense of fatherhood toward Navarro. But Romero was not forgiven for this difference (even during Borgonovo's funeral troubled murmurs arose in the church, as though Romero had been partly responsible for the murder). A false story was spread that a priest had celebrated a *Te Deum* after learning of Borgonovo's death. The major daily newspapers of the country reported the news of Borgonovo's death with full coverage and relegated the news of Navarro's death to the back pages. It clearly showed malice to treat the double homicide of a pastor and a parishioner as insignificant, especially since it happened in the center of the capital with clear signs of a terrorist vendetta. In any case, Borgonovo's death was a turning point, and members of the oligarchy started to distance themselves from Romero.

The *Misa Única*

On March 15, three days after Rutilio Grande's death, the clergy of San Salvador met and asked that all the priests concelebrate Mass in the cathedral the following Sunday morning, as a sign of unity. This was the *misa única*: that Sunday the faithful received a dispensation from the obligation to attend Mass in their parishes. Romero, skeptical at first, decided to accept this unusual request. After all, it did not violate the norms of canon law. The unity of the clergy was very important to him as bishop.

On March 16 Romero met with the nuncio, who was obstinately opposed to the initiative. Gerada asked him to change the decision he had made, and Romero became irritated with his insistence. In any case, Romero left the matter to the college of pastors of San Salvador, and a large majority confirmed the decision for the *misa única*. Romero wrote to Gerada about this, emphasizing his annoyance with the nuncio's intervention: "It seems to me that an archdiocesan matter is within the exclusive purview of the archbishop."

The *misa única* took place on March 20. One hundred thousand faithful poured in. It was a success, but it changed Romero's relationship with Gerada, who represented the Pope. This was one reason why Romero suddenly traveled to Rome on March 26. Paul VI recognized him at his Wednesday general audience and wished to receive him right away. In a fraternal spirit, he said something that became etched in Romero's mind and soul. It was the encouragement he needed, and he would repeatedly mention it later: "Take courage, you are in charge!" Romero later met with Father Arrupe, Superior General of the Society of Jesus; Cardinal Baggio, Prefect of the Congregation for Bishops; and then-Archbishop Agostino Casaroli, who handled relations between civil authorities and the Church at the Council for the Public Affairs of the Church, also known as the Holy See's Section for Relations with States. Romero recounted what had happened in his first month as archbishop of San Salvador, and they listened attentively. Complaints about him had not yet reached Rome. These would come later.

The conflict with Romero over the *misa única* was an unpleasant surprise for Gerada. He was not a man of extraordinary character. As a diplomat, he thought his primary task was to safeguard good relations between Church and State. He had hoped that Romero would be accommodating toward the government, and this was one reason he had supported his nomination. During his fiery initiation into his episcopal leadership role, Romero was especially annoyed by Gerada, who was trying to tell him what to do and what not to do. Gerada thought Romero was undoing his hard work of maintaining good relations with the government. The nuncio would soon become very critical of all of Romero's pastoral work, including his style of preaching. Gerada even went so far as to suspect him of being connected to the guerrillas, though he believed that personally Romero was a man of religious and moral integrity.

Conversion?

Rutilio Grande's death undoubtedly began to change Romero's attitude. A political and populist myth about Romero speaks of his changing from a conservative to become the moral leader of the Salvadoran people in the fight against military dictatorship and the oligarchy. According to this myth, Romero experienced a true conversion when confronted with the death of Rutilio Grande. This event transformed a backward, reactionary churchman into a champion of the people's struggle for liberation. Yet no such conversion appears in the writings and testimonies of many people who were close to Romero. His collaborators Jesús Delgado, Ricardo Urioste, and Gregorio Rosa Chávez do not describe the change that took place in Romero during his first days as archbishop of San Salvador as a sudden conversion. Romero's friends talk about a gradual change—he adapted to new responsibilities in a new historical situation. Rutilio Grande's murder was a decisive element in moving Romero to take responsibility for the poor and for the people who were hostage to violence, but it did not bring about a conversion in him. Rosa Chávez observed:

> It would be more accurate to say that *Monseñor* Romero underwent not a "conversion," strictly speaking, but an "evolution," as he himself said in a radio interview. This evolution was born of a

passion that always motivated the archbishop's journey: to discover God's ways and to respond generously to his calls. This is the natural evolution of someone who lives in an ongoing conversion, in total openness to God and to others.

Ricardo Urioste, Romero's vicar general, also disputed the idea that Romero had a sudden conversion:

> They ask me if there was some change in *Monseñor* Romero from the time of his ordination to Santiago de María to his years as archbishop in San Salvador. Yes, I think that there was a change, the change that God requires of every person, of every Christian, of every priest, of every bishop: to become ever more united to God, in a greater commitment to service, and to see reality and what this reality demands of a priest, a bishop. . . . *Monseñor* Romero was a man who always kept changing when the voice of God was calling him to do something. He discerned it in prayer, in conversation with God. He kept looking for what God was asking of him; *Monseñor* Romero reacted as the Gospel called him to. . . . His reaction was motivated to a great extent by the universal magisterium of the Church, by the magisterium of the popes . . . where it speaks of the Church's duty to defend human rights and to defend life. At that time, *Monseñor* Romero may not have been so daring, but seeing the Church's magisterium, he felt more courageous.

From 1972 onward, Romero had had bitter disagreements with the Jesuits of El Salvador. But somehow the murder of Rutilio Grande unexpectedly brought them closer again. Ellacuría's conduct was revealing in this regard. At first he was incredulous at Romero's reaction to Rutilio Grande's death. But as soon as he better understood his former adversary's position, he became extremely enthusiastic. The Jesuits of El Salvador instinctively believed that they were seeing the striking conversion of an enemy. In fact, they had disapproved of Romero's nomination as archbishop until the day before Rutilio Grande's death. This gave rise to the common idea of Romero's conversion.

His various biographers have dealt circumspectly with the idea that Romero had a conversion. But at the level of news reporting, polemics, popular narratives, and catch phrases, the commonplace of conversion was often used as part of the politicized myth about Romero. Héctor Dada Hirezi wrote: "This notion of Romero's conversion has been exaggerated, in some cases trying to show a radical change in his fundamental ideas. This goes beyond the realm of possibility for a man with Romero's spiritual experience." Dada Hirezi says that if we want to talk about a conversion by Romero, it is a conversion "like the one the Gospel demands of us: reading the Lord's message in everyday events and defining our actions on the basis of this reading. Starting from the same theological position, spirituality, and ideological approach, different circumstances will lead to different courses of action. This is especially true in the case of a bishop responsible for proclaiming and living the Gospel in a particular society and at a particular moment in time." Dada Hirezi talks about a change in Romero's "public attitude" but not in his faith.

Romero's clash with the government, which was persecuting the Church, was interpreted as a religious conversion. Instead it was Romero's acceptance of public responsibility. In a chaotic situation, he unexpectedly found himself in the role of the nation's ecclesiastical primate. For his part, Romero always denied having converted. Instead, he acknowledged changes in his conduct. During an interview in March 1979, when asked about his "conversion to the defense of human rights," he responded in the following manner:

> I would not talk about a conversion the way many do—if you wish to understand it that way—because I have always had affection for the people, for the poor person. Before becoming a bishop, I was a priest for twenty-two years in San Miguel. . . .

When I visited the cantons it was a real pleasure for me to be with the poor and to help them. Various small-scale projects were completed for their benefit while I served there as a priest. Upon arriving in San Salvador, however, the same fidelity with which I had tried to inspire my priesthood made me understand that my affection for the poor, my fidelity to Christian principles and loyalty to the Holy See had to take a slightly different direction. On February 22, 1977, I took possession of the archdiocese and on that day many priests were expelled. My predecessor, *Monseñor* Chávez, had already seen several priests violently exiled, which I could not prevent either. Less than a month after my installation, on March 12, 1977, the murder of Father Rutilio Grande occurred . . . At a meeting of priests we spent a day deliberating the stand that we should take with respect to the death of Father Rutilio Grande. It was a grace-filled day for me, since I understood the need to take a stand. In fact a decision was made: to celebrate just one Mass [in the cathedral] and not to permit [parish] Masses on the following Sunday. This decision cost me a lot, but it was something that had a strong impact on the diocese, and it helped me feel courageous.

In an animated discussion at CEDES in March 1978, Romero "explained his change of attitude once he held the office of archbishop because of changes in the situation, especially with the death of Father Grande a few days after Romero's installation in the archdiocese." This is how Romero responded to a journalist at the Puebla Conference who asked him how his "conversion" had happened: "You can call it a conversion if you like, but I think it would be more accurate to describe it as a development in the process of awareness. I have always wanted to follow the Gospel, even though I could not guess where the Gospel would lead me." Another journalist in Puebla asked him during the press conference whether he had "also converted to preaching about the poor," and Romero exclaimed, "If only I had converted!" The group reacted with laughter.

In a letter to John Paul II in early November 1978, just after the pope's election, Romero wrote about himself and especially about having strained his "conservative" nature. He did not talk about conversion, but rather a "special pastoral *fortaleza*" in a situation of conflict and persecution, of tortured and murdered priests and catechists, and of forcibly scattered Christian communities. The term *fortaleza*, which Romero also used on other occasions to explain his pastoral conduct, referred to fortitude, one of the four cardinal virtues in Catholicism:

> My transfer from the suffragan diocese of Santiago de María to this Metropolitan See coincided with an especially tragic hour of our ecclesiastical and national history. Thus my elderly predecessor hastened the time of the succession, which took place privately without the usual external solemnities. [Events included] the final months of a presidential term, which were characterized by marked political repression; the succession of a new president, who according to most of the people had been elected fraudulently and who continued human rights violations; and finally an entrenched situation of the sort the Latin American Bishops in Medellín justly described as a "situation of institutionalized injustice or violence." Because the Church was faithful to her mission of evangelizing by fostering the conscience of society and by denouncing the injustices and abuses of authority, all these things made the Church the central object of the persecution. . . . I believed in conscience that God was calling me and gave me a special pastoral fortitude that contrasted with my temperament and my "conservative" inclinations. I thought it was my duty to take a positive stand to defend my Church, and, on behalf of the Church, to stand with my greatly oppressed people.

What was chalked up as a conversion was not a transformation of Romero's faith. Romero did not change his fundamental ideas about God and Christian life. But he certainly adopted an attitude

of fortitude *(fortaleza)* in the crisis surrounding him. The significant new element in Romero's conduct was his attitude toward
political power (although as noted earlier, he had ongoing episodes
of conflict with civil authorities). This probably led to the commonplace idea of Romero's conversion, transferring something of an
entirely different sort to the religious sphere. Romero's previous attitude of avoiding conflict in his dealings with presidents and
ministers changed into an uncompromising stance demanding justice, first for Rutilio Grande and then—for over three years as a
bishop—for all of the crime, violence, and violations of human
rights in El Salvador. This transformation was interpreted as a conversion, but the term is inappropriate because it presumes that the
primary arena of faith is politics.

At a meeting in Rome on June 21, 1978, Baggio informed
Romero about some of the accusations against him in El Salvador.
Among other things it was said that Romero went around proclaiming that he had "converted," unlike the other Salvadoran bishops.
Romero denied ever having said that he had converted. Instead he
explained that he had experienced "a development of the desire I
have always had to be faithful to what God was asking of me. If I
gave the impression before of being more 'prudent' and 'spiritual' it
was because I sincerely believed that in that way I was responding to
the Gospel. The circumstances of my [previous] ministry did not
indicate the need for a pastoral *fortaleza*, which, in contrast, I
believe in conscience was required of me in the circumstances in
which I assumed the office of archbishop."

Romero as archbishop was different from the previous Romero.
That is clear. But Romero's faith did not change. His circumstances
and responsibilities changed, and so did the story around him. In a
national situation of crisis, Romero became the *defensor civitatis* in

accordance with the tradition of the Church Fathers. He defended persecuted clergy, protected the poor, and affirmed human rights. He felt the need to take up the legacy of love for the *campesinos* that he had admired in Rutilio. While keeping prayerful vigil for his murdered friend, Romero experienced inner emotion that moved him to make the poor one of the main reasons for his life. Rutilio Grande's death was at the root of Romero's interior change, which was a choice of *fortaleza* in defending the oppressed and the persecuted.

In demanding justice for his friend Rutilio, Romero found himself united with the diocesan clergy. He set aside his reservations about the orthodoxy of certain priests, about the politicization of the Jesuits, and about the *medellinismo* of the clergy.[2] As bishop in a difficult situation, he needed consensus. Above all he felt responsible for the safety of his priests. At that point the doctrinal clarity of individual priests or catechists was secondary. The crucial thing was that his priests and faithful were in danger of being murdered, so he had to defend them. It was the reaction of a bishop to the killing of his priests. Romero wanted to be a "good shepherd," which was his life's ideal. In this sense, his change fulfilled long-held personal aspirations. In order to understand Romero as archbishop, certain role models of pastors whom he admired should not be forgotten, such as Charles Borromeo and the more recent Pius XI, the pope during his early years in Rome. Both of them firmly opposed totalitarianism in its different forms. Like these two great pastors, Romero had a very lofty idea of the bishop's office.

---

2. The clergy had placed a fair amount of emphasis on ideas promoted by the 1968 Medellín Conference of CELAM. —*Trans.*

Persecution of the Church and Social Injustice

For three years Romero watched El Salvador's slow but steady slide toward civil war, alternating between times of acute crisis and relative calm. Repression fed the flames of guerrilla fighting and vice versa. The Salvadorans lived up to their bellicose reputation among the other countries of the isthmus. In El Salvador, the internal crisis was caught up with the winds of the Cold War blowing through Central America.

During this time the Church was persecuted. Most of Romero's priests were subjected to physical and psychological violence, and many catechists were killed. It became dangerous to own a Bible or a Gospel, especially in rural areas. Even a photograph of Romero or a copy of *Orientación*[3] were reasons enough for being murdered. In some areas people were killed just for going to Mass. This is how about fifteen people died in Chalatenango, and more would probably have perished but religious services were suspended.

During Romero's first four months as archbishop, at the end of Molina's presidency, about thirty priests of the archdiocese of San Salvador were attacked in various ways. Two were murdered, others were tortured, threatened, beaten, expelled, or forced into exile to avoid being killed. In this way the presbyterate of San Salvador lost about 15 percent of its active members. This was a serious loss for a Church suffering from a clergy shortage. Paid advertisements signed by fictitious associations constantly appeared in the press with accusations against the Church and threats against the clergy.

Little changed with the transfer of power to General Carlos Humberto Romero in July 1977. Three more priests were murdered

---

3. *Orientación* was the diocesan newspaper. —*Ed.*

and their faces disfigured out of extreme contempt ("Neto" Barrera on November 28, 1978, with two workers; Octavio Ortiz on January 20, 1979, with four boys; Rafael Palacios on June 20, 1979). The archbishop often received anonymous letters containing insults, threats, and accusations. Humiliations were frequent, such as body searches at checkpoints. While celebrating the funeral of a wealthy man killed by the guerrillas, Romero heard someone shout, *"Sacerdotes de Belcebú, vayan todos a Moscú."*[4] The congregation applauded.

In civil society, likewise, the change in presidential leadership produced no lasting solutions to the violence. The National Guard, the *Policia de Hacienda,* and the army, especially ORDEN, systematically carried out acts of suppression in the countryside. Sometimes this was in response to actions against property, and at other times it was for intimidation. The extrajudicial executions carried out by military and paramilitary groups with ties to the State and to landowner organizations routinely went unpunished. There were many *desaparecidos.*[5] The guerrilla opposition also used violence, including kidnappings, murders, sabotage, and damage to infrastructure. Those who took to the streets as *organizados* during public demonstrations brought weapons and were ready to brandish them at the opportune moment. In the countryside, rural labor unions victimized by the repression attacked those who sided with the landowners and the government. Romero received many pleas to make it publicly known that one citizen or another was not a member of right-wing organizations or a police force so that they would not be killed.

---

4. "All you priests of Beelzebub, go to Moscow." —*Trans.*

5. There were many "people who disappeared." —*Ed.*

Terror escalated on both sides. Whereas in 1978 about 150 politically motivated murders were recorded, in 1979 the count climbed to about 600 by October, when a coup d'état changed the situation again. Overall, the repressive violence of the regime—equipped with more powerful means of attack—was more serious and brutal in quantitative terms than the revolutionary violence. But each side provoked the other, aware of the escalation toward war. The guerrilla mentality of "so much the worse, so much the better" exalted the revolutionary ideal at the expense of the value of life. That mentality was the mirror image of the military intelligence mentality, which considered it necessary to eliminate at least 200,000 Salvadorans infected by Communism.

How did Romero react to this trend in the country? His fourth and final pastoral letter, dated August 6, 1979, is an important document in this regard. In the letter he identifies three "idolatries" that caused the crisis in the country: wealth, national security, and organization. Two were idolatries of the right, so to speak, and one of the left. The idolatry of wealth and private property left a vast segment of the population in conditions of unjust destitution. The idolatry of national security, invoked to ensure the oligarchy's interests through military intervention, reflected "the institutionalizing of the insecurity of individuals" and prevented democracy, which could have brought about social justice. By the "idolatry of organization" Romero meant the self-worship that the opposition groups tended to foster. It was not a critique of the right to form popular organizations and labor unions, which the Church in El Salvador had often defended, but a call to pursue the common good rather than the group's own success. Romero explained this form of idolatry in these terms: "I support all the just demands of these organizations. Nonetheless, when they abuse their power, when they claim what goes beyond justice, or when they act in what appears to be an imprudent or fanatical manner, I must say so. If they do not put themselves at the service of the people and the common good, but at their own service, I must denounce this."

According to Romero, the tragedy in El Salvador had its origins essentially in social injustice and was expressed with inhumane, unacceptable violence. In order to "have done with these violent situations, and with fruitless acts of terrorism," it was necessary to go to the roots of the national crisis. Those roots were in "permanent and institutionalized injustice that plunges the majority of our people into a state of subhuman destitution." Romero insisted on the necessity of just laws applied impartially: "It will be a just law only when it rewards the good of those who are above and those who are below, and when it punishes the evil of those who are below and those who are above." And so he preached:

> If it is true that terrorism and violence cannot be excused in the name of dissent, neither can officially sanctioned violence be justified. Such sanctions pervert the legal system, which is the sole means of assuring the survival of our traditions. . . . The safest way to defeat terrorism is to promote justice in our societies: legal, economic, and social justice. Summary justice undermines the very future that it intends to promote and produces only more violence and terrorism. Respect for the rule of law promotes justice and eliminates the seeds of subversion. In abandoning this respect, government leaders descend into the lower depths of the terrorist world and invalidate their most powerful weapon, their moral authority.

In his homilies Romero touched the heart of the country's problem, denouncing the widespread injustice, especially in the rural areas. He said the government had the greatest responsibility for this situation, because in ruling the country the government was supposed to set an example of respect for the laws that the citizens had to observe. Romero did not have an anti-establishment attitude. He did not imagine that institutions would be deprived of their authority based on vague concepts of popular power. Precisely because of his high esteem for institutions, he became indignant when they grew corrupt or when the purposes for which they existed were changed. His criticism of the government did not aim to destroy institutions, but to make them fair, impartial, and responsible. He was not scandalized by the Salvadoran political system in itself, but by "the hypocrisy, the distortion, the deception," the moral corruption that he found in government circles.

Romero often spoke of the need for solutions that were intelligent, rational, nonviolent, and in accord with justice. What did he mean? Romero was fond of the political idea of the patriotic unification of the healthy forces of the country, whether they came from the government or the people, from the right or the left, from the Christian Democrats or popular organizations. These forces needed to dialogue and unite with one another in order to achieve "a peace built on justice." Romero was constantly concerned, on the one hand, with stopping the bloody suppression of initiatives by unions and popular groups, and, on the other hand, with avoiding "an armed rebellion which, if unleashed in El Salvador, will truly be terrible."

These sparse indications did not amount to a political program, which Romero did not have. They did, however, express the line that Romero took publicly. The archbishop believed in more than just a political program. He believed in a spiritual advancement of all Salvadorans, both the people and the ruling classes. This is the theme of the "civilization of love," which Romero borrowed from Paul VI and often repeated. As Romero put it, the Church was the "builder of the community through love, and this distinguishes her from any other group or movement." When journalists asked about his solutions for El Salvador, he said that "this is what I have always preached: the best peaceful solution is a return to love and to a genuine desire for dialogue."

This profound response to the national crisis came from the Christian virtues: "work and prayer, which are man's strength"; the "spirit of poverty, which is a true solution to social injustice in our milieu"; and the "impartiality that clearly reveals certain extremist positions of our age as being irrational." Romero believed in the sanctifying and redeeming power of sacrifice and of the acceptance of pain and suffering: it was not politics but the redemption inherent in God's plan that could "change injustices by means of a more fraternal and just order." Romero preached that "the main thing is not a political solution . . . that will be added later." He explained:

> This is the greatness of Christianity: we do not live by the comings and goings of earthly conveniences. Therefore, addressing the dear Christian communities, I insist above all that they keep their faith in Christ; let them keep, above all, their transcendent character, and so let them illumine what is immanent and transitory. If we make a political judgment incorrectly, that does not matter; human beings are fallible. The important thing is not to be wrong in matters of faith. The important thing is to be faithful to the word of the Lord who guides all events. . . . This I ask of the Lord: "Grant us, O Lord, politicians, leaders, men who have faith!" A change of structures, no matter how profound, would do no good if those structures were not guided by men of faith.

Every Sunday from the pulpit Romero listed the violent events that had happened during the week. Given the distorted information provided by the government-friendly media, he believed that a more objective awareness of events would help to stem the violence. Thanks to the diocesan broadcasting station Radio YSAX, his voice was heard throughout the country. His homilies were rebroadcast several times, and Romero would add comments and interviews during the week. Radio YSAX had a very large audience: an estimated 73 percent of the population in the countryside and 47 percent in the cities. During one of Romero's Sunday broadcasts, which could be as long as two hours, it was possible to walk down the street without missing a single word, because in nearly every home a transistor radio was on. The segment dedicated to the news was certainly an attraction in such tragic and difficult times. But it should not be forgotten that Romero's homilies were mostly devoted to a commentary on the Scripture readings of the day. They were essentially religious homilies. Romero based his interpretation of the realities of life on the words of Scripture. He reexamined the crucial aspects of the crisis in El Salvador at the religious level, far from the political arena. For example, this is how Romero spoke about the spread of violent death and torture:

> The fifth commandment is brief but dreadful: "You shall not kill." Here the sacredness of human life is proclaimed. Remember that all this is under the heading: "I am the Lord your God, I who gave life and health to your brother, and you go and take it away from him." How much blood is obliterating happiness among us and the sanctity of this commandment! They order people to kill, they pay people to kill, and people earn money by killing. They kill to get rid of the political enemy who bothers them, and they kill out of hatred. . ... If only the men whose hands are stained with murder listened to me! Unfortunately, they are many! Someone who tortures is a murderer too! He who starts to torture does not know where it will end. We have seen victims of torture brought with a thousand false subterfuges to the hospital to die. Torturers are murderers too, for they do not respect the sacredness of life. No one can lay a hand on another human being, because man is the image of God. "You shall not kill!" I wish that this short saying could also affect this immense sea of disgrace.

Why was there killing? Why was there torture? Romero answered:

> God sowed goodness. No child is born wicked. All of us have been called to holiness. The values that God sowed in the human heart and that our contemporaries value so highly are not rare stones. . . . Why then is there so much wickedness? . . . The primordial, original vocation of the human being is to goodness. No one is born with inclinations to kidnap, to be a criminal, a torturer, or a murderer. We are all born to be good, to love one another, to understand one another. Why then, Lord, have so many weeds sprouted in your fields? The enemy did this, Christ says. Man has allowed his heart to be overgrown with weeds, bad companions, wicked inclinations, vices. . . . Yet we are all called to goodness. . . .

The Question of Violence

Romero acted and spoke out against violence, whatever its source. He was a meek, nonviolent person. Neutrality was nearly impossible in the polarized El Salvador of the time, yet Romero reasoned as a neutral party and spoke of forgiveness, not hatred. Those who encountered him without prejudice saw a man with peaceful intentions. Father Bartolomeo Sorge, who worked with him in Puebla, recalled:

> He explained to me the painful, tragic situation of his country, which he loved. He told me about the trampling of human rights, the disappearance of many of his sons, cases of torture and summary executions, the violent climate of repression that was driving El Salvador toward popular insurrection (so he feared). Nevertheless he did not have one word of hatred or rage. On the contrary, he firmly believed that the violence had to stop,

wherever it originated. He said that revenge had to be forbidden and that, in its place, justice in love had to triumph so as to achieve reconciliation and peace.

In one of his last homilies Romero said:

It is time for reconciliation. How much we, here in El Salvador, need to meditate a bit on this parable of the prodigal son! How irreconcilable they seem, the left's denunciation of the right and the right's hatred of the left. Those in the middle say: "Let the violence come from wherever it may; it is cruel in either case." So we live in polarized groups. Those in the same group may not even love one another, because love cannot exist where there is so much division that people hate each other. We need to break these barriers and to realize that we have a father who loves us all and is waiting for us all. We need to learn to recite the Our Father and to say to him: "Forgive us, as we forgive."

On the World Day of Peace in 1978, Paul VI chose and commented on the theme: "No to violence, yes to peace." Romero liked it very much. He made it his second motto, after *"Sentir con la Iglesia."* He agreed with the Pope about the existence of "two types of violence," which he interpreted in this way: "One springs from the frenzy for 'power' or possession, which destroys the lives of persons or society in order to maintain by force its own political structure and unjust organizations. The other arises out of resistance to the first—the violence of the weak, of those who are deprived of any fundamental rights." And he added concisely that "the devil puts sin into both types of violence."

The phrase "only love liberates" was often on Romero's lips. It expressed the idea that the solution of the nation's problems lay in the conversion of hearts rather than in politics, and certainly not in violence. Here are two citations from Romero's homilies during the Easter season in 1978:

The only legitimate violence [is] the violence that Christ does to himself and that he invites us to do to ourselves: "Let those who would follow me deny themselves," be violent to themselves, repress in themselves outbursts of pride, and kill in their heart outbursts of greed, avarice, conceit, arrogance. Let them kill this in their heart. This is what must be killed. This is the violence that must be done, so that out of it a new person may arise, the only one who can build a new civilization: a civilization of love.

And a few days later he said:

Brothers and sisters, it is necessary to throw away many idols, first of all the idol of ego, so that we may be humble. We can be redeemers, we can be co-workers in the true liberation that the world needs, only through humility. Liberation that is shouted at others is not true liberation. Liberation that brings about revolutions of hatred and violence, taking other people's lives or diminishing their dignity cannot be true liberty. True liberty does violence to oneself, like Christ. Refusing to be recognized as a sovereign, he made himself a slave to serve others. These are the true liberators, who in this momentous hour ask our country for humble hearts, hearts in which love shines as a Christian characteristic.

Only violence done to oneself[6] was legitimate. This sort of violence was "much superior" to that of weapons, because it was the violence of Christ on the cross. Romero said, "The only violence the Gospel allows is violence done to oneself. When Christ allows himself to be killed, this is violence: letting himself be killed. Violence done to oneself is more effective than violence done to others. It is

---

6. While one may never intentionally harm oneself, Romero here refers to the Christian understanding of self-sacrificing love, following the example of Christ. —*Ed.*

very easy to kill, especially when you have weapons, but how difficult it is to allow oneself to be killed for love."

He preached in a similar way during the Mass of the Lord's
Supper on Holy Thursday in 1978:

> To those of you who are devoted to violence and to vice and have
> now lost faith in love, thinking that love solves nothing, here is
> proof that only love solves everything. If Christ had wanted to
> impose redemption by the force of weapons or the force of arson
> and violence, he would have achieved nothing. It would have
> been useless: more hatred, more wickedness. But the crowning
> point at the heart of redemption is given to us on this night when
> he says to us: "This is my commandment: that you love one
> another as I have loved you. And so that you might see that these
> are not merely words, keep watch this night, this night during
> which I will sweat blood at the sight of the wickedness of men
> and the pain of my sufferings. Tomorrow when you see me pass
> by, as a silent lamb, with the cross on my shoulders to die on
> Calvary, know that I hold no grudge against anyone, that from
> the depths of my heart I am crying, 'Father, forgive them, for they
> know not what they do!'"

Civil war was looming. Many asked the archbishop about the
legitimacy of an armed rebellion against the government. The conviction spread that Romero considered a popular uprising justified
and inevitable. But this was an oversimplification. As Romero told
the press, he held in principle to the traditional Thomistic teaching that an insurrection would be legitimate, but only if "all
peaceful means had been exhausted" and if "the evils of insurrection [were] not worse than the evils of the dictatorship or
tyrannical power to be eliminated." He added that "the historical
application" of those principles did not fall under "the compe-
tence of the Church," but instead required consultation with
"experts in political science and strategy." In practice, Romero

believed there was an "institutionalized and repressive violence" in El Salvador that was opposed by "revolutionary violence." In striking back at one another, these two types of violence spiraled into death and ruin. For Romero, revolutionary violence was rooted in objective social injustice. The injustice had to be eliminated, rather than defended with "repressive violence." Although "the Church neither approves nor justifies bloody revolutions," she could nevertheless understand the reasons for them. Romero admitted that "while it is easy to formulate the ideal of peace, it is very difficult to confront the reality of violence that appears historically inevitable until its real causes are eliminated"; in other words, until the elimination of "a situation of injustice in which most men and women—and especially children—find themselves deprived of the necessities of life."

It was an analysis of reality, not a positive judgment about revolutionary violence. On the contrary, Romero described such violence pejoratively as "terroristic and seditionist": "It is a violence that produces and provokes fruitless and unjustified bloodshed; it creates tensions within society that are explosive and rationally uncontrollable, and on principle it disdains any form of dialogue as a potential means of resolving social conflicts." Just as he denounced repressive violence aimed at perpetuating injustice, so too he denounced violence in the name of justice: "This fanatical violence by certain groups or individuals that is becoming almost 'mystical' or 'religious' is doing great harm to our people. They divinize violence as the only source of justice. This pathological mentality makes it impossible to stop the spiral of violence." Yet when he condemned revolutionary violence he always also denounced the injustices that provoked it.

Romero was unequivocal in an interview in May 1979, a time of intense turbulence in the country: "As Paul VI also states in

Popolorum Progressio, theoretically, when there are no other means of reestablishing justice, even violent action may be permitted as a last resort. But we say this is not a just solution, since it can give rise to a veritable 'mysticism' of violence, which can only lead to other horrors. We are in favor of nonviolent opposition and a gradual transition to democracy, preferably without spilling blood."

Romero disapproved of all violence. Instead he proposed the power of spiritual deterrence against violence. As he said after the barbarous murder of Father Octavio Ortiz and of four young men with him:

> The battle of Christians is to be converted themselves and to convert the world from sin to the kingdom of God, which is already near . . . a battle that does not need tanks or machine guns. A battle that does not need a sword or a gun. . . . Because the Pope said that "violence, even when there are just reasons, is still violence and is neither effective nor dignified." Let those who, upon seeing such deeds, feel the natural instinct for revenge and violence learn to control themselves. Let them know that there is a kind of violence far superior to that of tanks or even that of guerrilla warfare. It is the violence of Christ: Father, forgive them, for they know not what they do; those poor souls are ignorant!

CHAPTER FOUR

Faith and Politics

The Clergy and Faithful of San Salvador

Romero governed the metropolitan archdiocese of San Salvador, which in 1978 had a Catholic population of 1,312,030. The other four dioceses in the country, taken together, had a Catholic population of 2,476,390 (Santa Ana, 864,000; San Miguel, 587,000; San Vicente, 565,000; Santiago de María, 460,390). A clergy census showed there were 229 priests in the archdiocese of San Salvador, 89 of them diocesan priests and 140 religious, most of whom were not Salvadoran. But in 1978 only 185 priests were in the diocese, because many had been expelled from the country. El Salvador had a ratio of 9,609 faithful per priest (7,092 in the archdiocese of San Salvador). During that same time,

Europe had an average of one priest for every 2,000 faithful. Given
the priest shortage, it is understandable that the idea of base communities was greeted enthusiastically in El Salvador, as it was
elsewhere in Latin America. These new groups were supposed to
make up for the lack of priests and for the geographical distances in
parishes covering hundreds of square kilometers [more than 100
square miles], with 20,000 or 30,000 souls entrusted to the care of
only one resident priest. The base communities seemed well suited
for evangelizing sectors of such vast parishes, supplying what was
lacking in the organized pastoral ministry.

In the archdiocese of San Salvador many priests subscribed to a
generic, Medellinist progressivism. In San Salvador this was grafted
onto the social Christianity of the forty-year diocesan rule of
Archbishop Chávez. What did it mean to be Medellinist? It meant
a preferential option for the poor, criticism of unjust social structures, the recognition of social sin as well as individual sin,
commitment to a militant Christianity, the call to *consciousness raising* and *change*, and being proud of the gifts Latin America brings to
the Catholic Church. This was the mindset of the Jesuits who, with
about fifty active members, had great weight in diocesan affairs. In
El Salvador, too, the Society of Jesus lived up to its reputation for
having members who were well-educated and well-prepared, who
stood out in contrast to the less extensively educated local clergy.
The Jesuits ran Central American University with its 3,500 students. The priests presented the institution as a place of "liberated
education ... at the service of the liberation process of the Salvadoran
people, which faces a situation of structural oppression." Moreover
they edited prestigious publications, directed Radio YSAX, headed
sectors of the diocesan Curia, and ran institutions, boarding schools,
and parishes. No archbishop of San Salvador could have done without their contributions, much less in times of crisis.

Other heavily politicized priests identified with the group called "*la Nacional.*" Although a minority, their presence was anything but subdued. For them, conversion meant dedicating oneself to social struggle, and faith had to be transformed into politics. They were inspired not so much by Medellín as by the "Christians for socialism," which originated in Chile. In 1977, few of them had ties to the guerrilla movement. But this changed after 1980, during the long civil war, when "*la Nacional*" would simply become "*Iglesia Popular,*" ["People's Church"] an alternative to the official Church.

Quite a few priests, however, disagreed with the politicization then in fashion. But they did not make their opinions known publicly for fear of having to swim against the current. The elderly priests of the archdiocese of San Salvador in particular felt uneasy about the political ferment and the atmosphere of direct confrontation with the government, preferring a classical pastoral approach, a sacramental approach. Finally, a good number of priests openly sympathized with the oligarchic right. These priests gave priority to politics over faith in the same way as the priests of "*la Nacional,*" siding with the oligarchy instead of the revolution.

The laity of the archdiocese of San Salvador reflected the various positions of the clergy. A certain type of sociological uneasiness could be observed in the work of the parishes: the laity had to become involved according to plans and methods, criteria and levels, tactics and objectives, priorities and guidelines. The religious message was a mixture of the old and the new. Popular religiosity and militant faith, pious practices and calls to action, lived side by side. Sacramental ministry did not exclude ideological appeals to *raise consciousness*. Traditional devotions continued, but so did apocalyptic fears of persecution.

With respect to Romero's work, his conservative principles, and his passionately prophetic words, most of the faithful were in favor of him, although not unanimously. As a whole they suffered from the oligarchy's hatred of the Church. They were surprised to see such outrages against religion as had never before occurred in El Salvador. So it was a relief for them to see in the archbishop a high spiritual and moral standard to look up to. Even traditionally-minded associations felt that they had to speak out in favor of greater justice in the country, as Romero asked. They did so in a language that was quite different from that of liberation theology. A group of Knights of Christ the King wrote to Romero, invoking the most abundant divine blessings upon the archbishop: "We know that the Church is working to bring about a more just society." The letter continued: "Pius XII said that God does not want some to have excessive wealth and others to be in such straits that they lack the necessities of life. In other words, God does not will the shameful contrast between wasteful luxury and destitution. God does not want destitution. God created the goods of the earth for all humanity and he wants all to possess those goods." Similarly the Militia of Christ the King, with its crusading language, fervently declared to Romero its commitment to fight against vice, sin, alcohol, prostitution, egotism, and Communism—"the devil's instrument"—but also against injustice. It condemned the idea "that the only thing that matters is money."

As archbishop, Romero received thousands of letters, notes, and messages from simple lay Catholics, who were often semi-illiterate. Events such as Romero's birthday (August 15), the prizes or international honors he received, his trips to Rome, or the death of Paul VI became occasions for them to write to the archbishop, giving free vent to their feelings. They turned to Romero not only as their bishop, but also as the Pope's representative in El Salvador, as the father of the country, as the physician of the people's anxieties, as an oracle to consult for solutions, or as a prophet offering hope.

Romero's mail was a barometer of his popularity. Some praised Romero to the skies in ornate terms. He is "a great apostle, prophet, and pastor who by risking his own life is leading us along the paths of salvation." He is "truly a prophet, John the Baptist [of the] Savior." He is "the greatest man of all times in these parts," called to "vanquish this beast that is trying to trample down our Christian religion." He is "an apostle of God," "a man of Providence." A large amount of poetry was dedicated to Romero and sent to him in the letters. In these lyrical, amateur, and popular pages, Romero is glorified above all as a prophet of *verdad* [truth]. This term *verdad* is found in many letters received by Romero. This was a sign of the people's confidence in him and also in the Gospel, because this *verdad* is connected with Romero's preaching of the Gospel.

The letters to Romero have a predominantly religious tone and have only a few references to political parties, tactics, and strategies. They often relate personal incidents. Here and there one finds lamentations over the apocalyptic "beast," understood as evil, corruption, misgovernment, and the persecution of the Church and the farmers. A group of prisoners writes:

> We had the opportunity to listen to your valuable program broadcast by Radio YSAX. We think that through this program you will be able to change our conscience toward a better life. If we compare your program with the other commercial programs, we realize that those are what led us to perdition, since they urge us with the old songs, "Let's take another drink!" That is the crime that brought us here. That is why we had to leave our children and our wives out in the cold; this is what led to robberies, crimes, acts of violence, and offenses against our friends and family members. *Señor* Archbishop, given what we are experiencing here in this detention center, we pray to God that decent programs like this one of our Church will be broadcast someday by all the media so that, just as we are already thinking about a decent life, our people can do the same.

The letter writers often speak about consolation, grace, forgiveness, and conversion. They ask for advice about reciting the Rosary, offer donations for the diocese and for the poor, seek recommendations, present family matters, or ask questions about the faith. Often they praise the Pope, who is seen together with Romero as a bulwark against evil. The humbler the correspondent, the more profound is his devotion to the Pope and the more affectionate his personal feelings for Romero. They are pleased with Romero's Church, which is following "its genuine path of humility and justice at the side of the disinherited." These gentle statements are far from the lofty rhetoric of the *organizados*. When the latter write, they applaud Romero in a similar way for a Church "alongside the oppressed," but they like to add ideological slogans. They repeatedly say that "to opt for the oppressed means to take a stand in their struggle," and that the Church which is committed to the people can be sure of "victory." The letters to Romero from the base communities, militant organizations, and consciousness-raising groups read like manifestos in class warfare, repeating expressions such as "We are at your command!"

The strictly personal letters that Romero received were quite different. They often describe the experience of evil, suffering, persecution, and blood. Thus a semiliterate peasant wrote:

> Reverend *Monseñor*, I did all that you told me in your letter. I read the Gospel from the Book of Saint Matthew and I started thinking about and analyzing everything the Gospel says. I also did what it tells me I ought to do, and I am trying to do it. *Monseñor*, now I want you to answer some questions. Why did people foment hatred, revenge, wickedness, injustice, hostility, and revenge killings? And why can't the better person establish peace, justice, and everything good? When God came to earth and saved us from our sins, he told us, or better, left us love, that we might love one another and live as friends—he left us all that

is good. *Monseñor,* why is it that people do evil but not good? And I ask myself whether the good causes are really so good because they prefer to take their own revenge.

Critical letters also arrived on Romero's desk. Usually anonymous and filled with threats, insults, abuses, and vulgarity, these short letters were written in the strident style of the right-wing culture. Or else they were furious, ranting letters without any logic. Instead of the usual cursive handwriting, the writers often preferred printed capital letters. They dabbled confusedly in their own ideas, made accusations, and used obscene language. They often made threats. They condemned Romero as a subversive, a Communist, because he was upsetting the fundamental balance of society divided between rich and poor, as established by God and nature. Although all are children of God—they write—not all are equal. Some are virtuous persons and some are criminals. The rich have worked to become rich. They sweated more than the others, and they are blessed by God who gave them their success. The rich are more generous than the poor, and they are worthy members of society because they give work to the poor, even though the latter have no desire to work.

Hope as Ideology

Much talk about base communities went on in Romero's particular Church. In these lively circles, justice and politics were discussed at length. *Raising consciousness* was considered the essence of conversion. This created an almost automatic process: faith was *raising consciousness,* and *raising consciousness* was political involvement, and finally, to complete the circle, political involvement was militant solidarity in the struggle for change, even to the point of revolution. The pastoral opportunity presented by the base communities was often transformed into an ideological phenomenon. It was no accident that expressions commonly used in those communities, such as "ideological level," "ideological criterion," "ideological content," and "ideological struggle," had a positive connotation. In other words, it was about following the right ideology. Members routinely professed their allegiance to Romero as "followers of his ideologies."

Many members of the base communities belonged to rural labor unions. Originally these had been Christian, but in the sixties they had embraced an openly political agenda that went beyond labor relations. Their publications were marked by a fighting spirit, symbolized by frequent stylized images of peasants brandishing machetes, and by their stereotyped language. Nothing was more natural than for the "exploited, oppressed people" and the "working class" victoriously to wage their "steadfast battle" against the "Creole bourgeoisie," "Yankee imperialism," and "fascistic military tyranny," to cries of *"Hasta la victoria siempre!"*[1]

These labor unions were incorporated into a political organization, the Popular Revolutionary Bloc. That in turn was connected with a guerrilla movement. Thus a member of the base communities who wanted to could make his way directly to the armed opposition, similar to a series of nested boxes. This was well known to the repressive organizations of the regime, which mentally ran through in reverse the organizational-ideological path taken by someone who had become a guerrilla fighter. They traced it back to the priests and catechists of the base communities, who, without directly pursuing either politics or armed conflict, had set up the

---

1. "Until everlasting victory!" —*Trans.*

consciousness-raising mechanism in the first place. This is why the base communities ran so cruelly afoul of the violence by the paramilitaries and by the savage operations of the legal military corps. In turn that mechanism fueled in those same communities a mystique of martyrdom and sacrifice for the revolution.

In the archdiocese of San Salvador the base communities were widespread, especially in the countryside. Their significance was in proportion to the fact that in 1977 only 44.3 percent of Romero's flock lived in rural areas. The base communities enjoyed a good reputation, recalled the early Christian communities, and boasted of their popular character. But that did not mean that they dominated the diocesan religious scene. The urban environment was not very receptive to the model that they proposed. The members of the base communities were mostly farmers, simple people. They received the message of the Medellinist-minded priests and catechists as a blueprint for life. The kingdom of God had to come about in their redemption from economic and political oppression. Not all the communities, however, became quite so radical. In the parish in Ilopango, Father Fabián Amaya defended the primacy of religion. He saw the base communities as places of biblical prayer and love for the poor and as an element that would bring order into the everyday family and social life of the persons who belonged to them. The people were called upon, for example, to regularize their marital unions and to avoid excessive drinking.

Romero supported the base communities. He liked them because of their popular character and their apostolate among the peasants and the poor. He took care to maintain personal contacts, as much as possible, with the individual communities. For their part they constantly sent appeals and messages to him. He noted with satisfaction the evangelical and social commitment of their catechists. At the same time, Romero wanted to avoid distorting religious teaching into a political agenda. Various passages from Romero's *Diary* attest to this. He stated in November 1979: "Being Christian is the primary thing. On this basis every believer must find his place in the country, according to the vocation that he has received from God. If God gave him a political vocation, let him live it out as a Christian." Romero took as his inspiration *Evangelii Nuntiandi* [On Evangelization in the Modern World] by Paul VI. This document emphasized at some length the ecclesial character of the base communities and warned against drifting into politics. In March 1980 a journalist pointed out to Romero that "the ecclesial base communities are accused of scattering seeds of insurrection." He replied: "'Ecclesial' means to make the Church. The base communities are nourished by the Gospel, by the sacraments, by transcendence: by everything that makes a human being truly Christian. And one Christian dimension is the political. Therefore, political engagement can be found in the base communities too." The journalist insisted and asked him again whether the base communities were committed to revolutionary efforts. Romero replied laconically: "As base communities, no," meaning that the communities were ecclesial entities and if one of their members was involved in revolutionary activity, it was as a private person. During his last spiritual exercises, a few weeks before he was killed, Romero included in an examination of conscience the fact that he had disregarded the politicization of the base communities.[2]

Romero defended the freedom for all to be active in labor unions or political activity. He considered it a basic right of citizens. He wanted Christians who were committed—as he said—to bringing "the redemption of Christ into the midst of the world."

---

2. Recorded in a spiritual notebook that Romero kept on his retreats. —*Ed.*

Nevertheless the spheres of the Church and of politics had to be quite distinct. He asked the faithful not to remain aloof from social and political problems. But at the same time he did not want them to confuse the field of the Church's action with that of politics:

> Faith and politics must be united in a Christian who has a vocation to politics, but without identifying one with the other. The Church wants both dimensions to be present in the life of Christians as a whole. Therefore she has had to recall that a faith separated from life is not true faith. But she also warns that the work of faith cannot be identified with a particular political task. The Christian with a political vocation must try to achieve a synthesis between Christian faith and political action, but without identifying the two. Faith must inspire the Christian's political action without being confused with it.

An atmosphere of constant emergency prevailed. Romero was constantly compelled by circumstances to react to unforeseen events. He could hardly dedicate himself to ordinary pastoral ministry. He had to defend the Church together with the people, especially the rural population, which was more exposed to outrages and violence. Family members of persons who had been arrested, tortured, or had simply disappeared called on him incessantly at the chancery. Sometimes he had to go to police headquarters to obtain the release of detainees. Family members of victims of guerrilla warfare also sought his help. The authority that he had acquired made him an indispensable mediator when situations had to be resolved, such as kidnappings, occupations of buildings and institutions, strikes and labor conflicts, or demonstrations. Romero was called on to add his efforts to those of the civil authorities. He did not shirk this task. No one should be left without help.

Nevertheless he was accused of being indulgent with the popular organizations on the left. Why did he not condemn the ongoing occupations of churches? In reality Romero never intended to tie himself and his local Church to any one political option, and he feared the politicization of the clergy and of the base communities. Several weeks before he was assassinated, after having experienced the hostility of the right and also of the left because of his public stances, he declared:

> Some have treated me as a Communist; others today consider me a traitor. . . . I run the risk that every preacher of the truth runs— that what he says will be misinterpreted, that he will be slandered, that he will be persecuted. Nevertheless I have confidence. . . . The Church does not identify herself with any movement, any party, any organization. . . . A bishop is not a politician. My perspective is pastoral and is based on the Gospel.

In a homily in May 1979, he explained his view that the Church was the conscience of society: "Christian love surpasses all kinds of regimes and systems. If today it is democracy, tomorrow socialism, and later something else, that is not the concern of the Church. It is up to you, the people—you who have the right to organize with the same freedom all nations have! Organize your social system; the Church will always remain on the sidelines, autonomous, so as to be the conscience of any system." How could the Church perform this function of conscience? Romero pointed out one criterion as a guideline. On February 17, 1980, he preached:

> I do not want to describe in minute detail all the ins and outs of politics in my country. I preferred to explain to you the deep roots of the Church's activity in this explosive world of Salvadoran social politics. I tried to make clear to you the ultimate theological and historical criterion of the Church's activity in this regard: the world of the poor. Depending on how it may go for them, for the poor people, the Church will support, in her specific way as Church, one or another political project. In other words, she will support the project that benefits the poor.

In his public speeches Romero denounced attacks on human life and called for justice for the poor, a truly large group in El Salvador. In doing so, we see from his writings and speeches that he based his reasoning on Catholic doctrinal heritage: the papal magisterium; social doctrine; Vatican II documents, especially *Gaudium et Spes*; and the texts composed at Medellín and Puebla.

Romero's adversaries most often accused him of engaging in politics. Let us allow Romero himself to respond: "What I seek to do is by no means politics. And if, because of the needs of the moment, I shed light on the politics of my fatherland, I do so as a pastor, in terms of the Gospel." The following passage from a homily given on August 6, 1977, expresses well Romero's approach to politics:

> The Church does not preach hatred but love. And if her words are sometimes violent, it is to uproot the reign of sin and to convert people to the Lord. The Church is not Marxist, and she is not committed to any social system. . . . The Church defends the ethics of her religion, of her love for God, and this is what interests her in any system whatsoever. Not becoming Marxist or capitalist, but telling the Marxists and the capitalists to convert from their materialism, so as to worship with her the one true God and to transform their social unrest into an eagerness to build up the true kingdom of God, which makes us feel that we are brothers with everyone. . . . Civil authority has its autonomy. And the Church too has its autonomy. They must collaborate for the common good, each one in its sphere. This is the Church's great polity: the common good. And because of her moral office in the world, she has the right to denounce the abuses of politics.

In his pastoral ministry, Romero was anxious to prevent politics from prevailing over the religious dimension. In March 1980 a journalist asked him whether the Church was acting as a "political substitute." A disillusioned Romero replied that there was already too much politics: "In San Salvador political awareness is already very strong. Here, people are political before they are Christian. The Church's task is to Christianize politics."

"Boundlessly Political," in Spite of Himself

In Romero's local Church a sort of ideological storm was brewing: the relation between faith and politics. Many Christians identified the kingdom of God with revolution, according to the typical language of the day. Even Romero believed that the kingdom of God started with earthly life. He wanted justice, especially for the poor. But he did not argue about revolution.

The meetings, assemblies, and even spiritual exercises of the diocesan clergy dealt with clarifying the relation between faith and politics, between the Church and current political events. (They never arrived at a final definition.) Different opinions were debated. Romero accepted these discussions, imposed by agendas that were not always his own. But he was glad when they went on to speak about "fraternity," "communion," and "human qualities." If he was called on to talk specifically about religion and politics, Romero insisted on priestly and ecclesial identity. He did so at the monthly meeting of the diocesan clergy in June 1979, after much discussion about politics:

> The last presentation fell to me and I tried to congratulate them for the richness of their contributions, to express the value of this kind of reflection, and to summarize in a few words all those terms: *clarification, Church identity, priestly unity*, (in order to present the mystery of our presbyterate as the nucleus and focus that illumines the Church's activity) and *discernment* (so that the Holy Spirit can give us the capacity to not confuse the Church with other lines of thought, and to authentically be Church, and

know how to understand others from the starting point of our own identity.)

On the eve of his death Romero was concerned about the "politicization" and "polarization" in his clergy, separating some of priests from others, as he noted in his *Diary*. He discussed with his collaborators the possibility of a new survey among the clergy to help "neutralize" the "reasons for division." He disapproved of "those socio-political aspects that often divide us or do not allow us to work together." He would invoke "clerical unity" on "the basis of human trust, friendship, and sincerity" regardless of "different currents of thought." Romero was severe with priests he suspected of having become political activists. He wrote to Placido Erdozaín, a priest originally from Spain involved in the popular organizations:

> Although I commend your intention to identify with the just aspirations of the working class, I wish to take this occasion to express my concern and to ask for your cooperation in order to avoid repeating things of which I cannot approve. Such things occurred during the Mass that you celebrated in the Léon Factory on Saturday the twenty-fourth: without chalice, without missal, without candles. But above all I ask myself: will there be true communion of faith with a group that is more pleased with its symbol of a fist held high than with the sign of the cross? Moreover some expressions about the "struggle of the people" seem ambiguous to me. I would be grateful for an in-depth discussion with you so that you might be in clear agreement with the pastoral policies of this Archdiocese. I ask you that the unity of our prayer for one another might help us to uphold the authentic authority of the Church, so as to proclaim on behalf of God the transcendent message of liberation.

In a letter to Bishop De Smedt of Bruges, Belgium, who had twinned his diocese with San Salvador by sending him several mission priests, Romero expressed the same opposition to the clergy's political involvement. The subject of the letter was Rogelio Ponseele, pastor in Zacamil:

> For some time now we have noted that Father Rogelio has taken initiatives and positions that clearly revealed his personal involvement with certain popular political organizations—not just the ministry of accompanying them so as to strengthen their faith. . . . As a result my confidence in him is greatly diminished, and his pastoral work is the cause of much anxious concern. . . . Therefore I ask you to call him back to work in his diocese of Bruges.

Romero favored the political involvement of the laity. But he said they must not embrace violent methods and had to recognize the priority of the religious over the political dimension. This was not easy in a bloody, mangled, overwrought country like El Salvador. Romero regarded the popular organizations on the left with respect and sympathy, insofar as they presented claims that were useful for the common good. He had no objection to militant Christians and defended their right to free association. But on many occasions he warned about the risks that the organizations seem to run: self-idolatry, sectarianism, taking politics as an "absolute," drifting into violence and terrorism, lack of respect for the religious sentiments of the people, and even manipulation of the Church. Romero was unyielding about violence: this was the sorest point in his relations with the popular organizations. He thought that, all told, the unjust social order defended by repressive forces was the most serious violence. Indeed, Romero did not develop an argument about opposed extremist ideologies; he did not propose a middle way. He maintained that El Salvador's problems were rooted in a grave social injustice— wealth in the hands of a few and the masses in miserable conditions—and that it was necessary to do away with this injustice.

Romero thought that a Latin American socialism could have different characteristics from the Soviet or Chinese systems. But that does not mean that he was in favor of Marxism. As a matter of principle, it was clear that both Marxism and capitalism were ruled out in Romero's thought:

> The Church cannot become an accomplice of any ideology that tries to create here on earth the kingdom in which human beings will be completely happy. Therefore the Church cannot be Communist. Nor can the Church be capitalist, because capitalism too is short-sighted, seeing its happiness, its passion, its own heaven in lands, mansions, money, in earthly things. These systems are set. And this set-up is incompatible with the Church. The Church is eschatological. And here the Church turns to the poor to tell them: you are the ones best able to understand this hope and this eschatology. . . . Communism falsely accused us when it told us that we preached the opium of the people and that, by preaching a kingdom in the next world, we took away from people their incentive to struggle on this earth. But which one gives more incentive to humanity, Communism or the Church? The Church, because in preaching the hope of heaven she tells people that this heaven must be merited, and in the measure in which they work here and perform their duties well, they will be rewarded for all eternity.

Romero did not take a middle-of-the-road position in Salvadoran society. He was aligned with the diverse part of society that was motivated by different ethical premises but still agreed in wanting to remedy social injustice. This does not mean that Romero belonged to the left. He regarded the serious problems of El Salvador from a traditional Christian perspective. He expressed the classic thought of Christianity concerning wealth, justice, and the poor. He wrote in his last pastoral letter:

To make wealth an absolute is to situate the human ideal in "having more" and therefore to diminish interest in "being more," which ought to be the ideal of the true progress of humanity and of the people. The absolute desire to "have more" promotes selfishness, which destroys the fraternal coexistence of the children of God. Therefore, this idolatry of wealth prevents the majority from benefiting from the goods that the Creator made for everyone, and it leads the minority that possesses everything to an exaggerated enjoyment of these goods.

God was found among the poor, the humble, and the weak. Even politics should take this into account. Thus Romero preached on Christmas in 1979:

Christ, the poorest of all and wrapped in swaddling clothing, is the image of a God who lowered himself—what theology calls *kenosis*. . . . Tonight let us not look for Christ in the opulence of the world, amid the idolatry of wealth, amid the desire for power, amid the intrigue of the great. God is not there. Let us seek God . . . among the undernourished children who have gone to bed tonight with nothing to eat. [Look for him] among the poor newsboys who will sleep each night covered with newspapers in doorways. [Look for him] in poor shoeshine boy who maybe has earned enough to get a little gift for his mother . . . or in the young peasant worker, who has no job, the one who is sick tonight. Not everything is full of joy. There is much suffering; there are many broken homes, there is much pain, and there is much poverty. Brothers and sisters, let's not look at all this with demagogy.[3] The God of the poor has assumed all that and is teaching [us] the redemptive value of human pain—the value that poverty, suffering, and the cross have to redeem the world. There is no redemption without the cross.

---

3. This seems to refer to an agitated, reactionary, or revolutionary spirit. —*Ed.*

> God does not want social injustice . . . God calls for justice, but
> he tells the poor carrying their cross, what Christ says to the
> oppressed: you will save the world if you give to your sorrow not
> the conformism that God does not desire, but rather a restlessness
> for salvation. . . . This is the Christ that is born, teaching poor coun-
> tries, those in the "inns", on these cold nights during the coffee
> harvest, or the hot nights near the cotton fields, all of that has
> meaning. . . . If there is something that I pity at this hour in which
> El Salvador is being redeemed, it is to think that many false redeem-
> ers risk losing the power of redemption available to our people:
> their suffering; and turn their marginalization, their hunger into
> demagogy. It should not be turned into desperation nor resent-
> ment, but wait for God's justice. . . . If there were not so much
> demagogy and if there were more holiness among the poor, our
> country would soon see salvation. . . . Let's give to earthly things
> their relative value. Let's not make wealth, struggles, the party, nor
> the organization an absolute. Nothing has absolute value on this
> earth; everything is relative in the face of the only Absolute.

Romero was not well acquainted with Marxism. He knew little
about sociology and philosophy. Even during his three years as archbishop, his readings were primarily magisterial, patristic, exegetical,
and devotional. As his guide in politics, he took the documents of
Vatican II on the relation between the Church and the world. He
knew that he was not an expert in politics. He was ironic about this:
"The problem in this country is that the two men who are confronting each other [Archbishop Romero and the President, General
Romero] not only have the same name, but also have in common
that neither one is a politician."

As the international journalists who worked in El Salvador saw
it, Romero's words carried great political weight. His positions
served as political guidelines, and his actions signaled a political
orientation. Romero was the pointer indicating the strategic balance of the country. The journalists were reporting an obvious

truth: Romero was the central figure in the public life of El Salvador. Every Sunday, his homilies served as a barometer for the country. With a few words he could orient the masses of people. Any action by Romero had strong political repercussions, but that does not meant he intended to engage in politics. He didn't act as a politician. Many of his friends and acquaintances think that he was incapable of engaging in politics in the technical sense. He was rather naive about the everyday dealings of politics. In private, people who came to speak to him could easily obtain his consent if they could attune themselves to his concerns, even if superficially. He had a straightforward logic, however, and he couldn't be fooled for long. Sooner or later the sincerity of his interlocutors was proved by deeds. In any case, Romero acted as a bishop, not as a politician. In a situation like El Salvador's, the very fact that he was not a politician paradoxically gave him a certain authority.

Romero took no offense when critics denied his political qualifications, for he had no ambitions of being a politician. Lucia Annunziata, who often met him in San Salvador, made the insightful remark that he was "boundlessly political, in spite of himself." Romero had no desire to be a leading political figure in his country. He wanted El Salvador to have a capable political class, and he did not want the Church take on roles substituting for the State. Due to circumstances, the light that Romero's homilies shed on the country's problems, with a view to finding solutions, became a central element of the Salvadoran political debate. In a way, Romero found himself supplying what was lacking in a deficient political class.

In October 1979, Duarte returned from exile in Venezuela. He then met Romero and told him that now he could finally stop worrying about being a political substitute, since Duarte saw prospects of democratic reforms in the country: "I will take up what you have done thus far; I will do in politics what you have had to do as a substitute. Now you can restrict yourself to your natural role." Like Duarte, many people had the sense that Romero was remedying the deep divide that existed between institutions and citizens, between the ruling class and the masses of the people. Romero lent himself to this endeavor out of a sense of responsibility, not because he wanted to engage in politics. He knew that he was not a master of that art. He also knew that he was bound in an impossible situation, between a right wing that would not hear of social justice and a left wing that would not hear of reform. The right wanted the status quo and the left wanted revolution. Yet these ideological clashes that led to civil war did not make him resigned or desperate. Beyond all logic or reason, Romero had faith and hoped for the impossible.

The majority of diplomats who were accredited in El Salvador had great esteem for Romero on the human and religious levels, but they considered him cumbersome and harmful on the political level. The U. S. embassy was courteous to the archbishop but avoided having him as a political partner. During Carter's presidency, however, the line taken in Washington with regard to El Salvador was no different from Romero's ideas: stability in the country, social justice, human rights, progress without Communism. Yet the North Americans decided that it was better not to engage in politics with Romero, because Romero did not reason as a politician.

Here is the Romero paradox: although he was not a politician and didn't want to engage in politics, being unskilled in that field, he found himself a key figure in the politics of his country. Compared with the average Latin American bishop, including the Salvadorans, Romero was not very inclined to politics. As a prelate, he was faithful to the Holy See's attempt to depoliticize the Latin American local churches in the name of the primacy of religion. Yet in El Salvador, as in other Latin American countries, the traditional

Spanish concept of civil life remained imprinted on customs: "the sword and the cross." The Church was the only authority that could substitute for or oppose the civil authority. Because of the Roman formation that he had received, Romero distinguished between the sword and the cross, State and Church, politics and religion. Nevertheless the context in which he found himself made him immediately the rival of the civil authority, not by laws but by virtue of a way of thinking. Thus he became a "boundlessly political" figure in spite of himself.

CHAPTER FIVE

"Sentir con la Iglesia"[1]

The Bishop of the Poor

Romero adhered to the spirit of Vatican II in the hope it would foster the unity of the archdiocese. However, he knew he was in charge of a pluralistic diocese. Some factions were stubbornly opposed to a pastoral approach based on Vatican II, and other sectors operated "at the other extreme, thus causing distrust." He was willing to accept a situation of

---

1. "To think with the Church," in Latin, *sentire cum ecclesia*. This phrase derives from Saint Ignatius, meaning to be of one mind and heart with the Church. —*Ed.*

"healthy pluralism in which all trends can coexist," provided that
they converged on a common plan of *cura animarum* [the care of
souls]. In any case, Romero was proposing to all sides, the clergy and
the faithful, a message of conversion that he hoped would foster the
unity of the archdiocese. According to Romero, the criterion of
genuine conversion was love for the poor, who represented Christ,
and this love obtained forgiveness and grace from God. But it was
also necessary to become poor, at least in spirit: "The poor person is
not only someone who does not have anything, but also someone
who knows how to own property according to God's will and love
of neighbor." In January 1979 the clergy of San Salvador discussed
the "true concept of poverty" and Romero spoke as follows:

> I expressed my opinion that everything was a matter of conver-
> sion, that a poor person is the one who had been converted to
> God and completely trusted in him, and that a rich person is the
> one who has not been converted and made money, power, and
> earthly things his idols. And that all our work should be about
> being converted ourselves and converting others to that sense of
> authentic poverty. Because Christ said that the secret lies in the
> fact that one cannot serve two masters, God and money.

Archbishop Romero desired Christian communities "in which
all our trust is placed in God . . . without the false pride of those who
think that they get their strength from worldly things. True poverty
is caring in a preferential way for the poor as though they were our
own concern. And therefore to feel that we ourselves are poor and
we need strength from God in all situations." He was thinking of a
"Church of the poor":

> You see, the Church of the poor is not a Church of demagogy. It
> is a Church that follows the pope and the Gospel and thus discov-
> ers its preference and its work for those most in need, drawing
> from it the strength to call for the conversion of all people. No

one will be saved without converting according to the words of Christ at the last judgment: "Whatsoever you did to one of these needy ones, you did to me."

Romero's pastoral approach kept its traditional character, although he took care to update the meaning of the classical devotions along conciliar lines. Romero was very devoted to the Blessed Virgin Mary. In a Mass celebrated for the mothers of the *desaparecidos* he declared Mary their model: "From the beginning, that is, from when she presented her Son in the temple, Mary was told that a sword would pierce her soul." He continued:

> No one has suffered as Mary did, because none of you mothers bore during her whole life a prophecy as Mary did from the time she rocked her baby in her arms. None of you mothers heard at the beginning of your own children's life a prophecy that announced to you the terrible, bloody end of your sons. If a mother knew from her son's infancy, as Mary did, that he would die tragically and that her own heart would be pierced by a sword, brothers and sisters, the whole life of that mother would be a Calvary and suffering. Mary, therefore, is the model of mothers who suffer. . . . Here is the secret, brothers and sisters: sorrow is useless when it is suffered without Christ, but when human sorrow continues Christ's sorrow, it becomes a sorrow that continues to save the world. It is like Mary's sorrow: a serene sorrow full of hope. Even when all despaired at the hour when Christ died on the cross, Mary serenely awaited the hour of the resurrection.

Romero developed the classic traits of the good bishop according to the Council of Trent: closeness to the clergy, attention to the unity of the diocese, concern for the seminarians, adherence to the magisterium, frequent pastoral visits, scrupulous application of canonical discipline and liturgical decorum, attachment to the cathedral, compassion for the sick, charity toward the poor. Archbishop Romero was in the first place a priest: he loved to celebrate Mass, talk about God, communicate his message to the faithful, and promote prayer and devotion. He had a fatherly disposition. After a meeting with a young priest, he noted: "I was touched by his sincere admission of feeling very happy in his first months of priesthood." He was enraptured by the themes of the liturgical feast days, always the same on the calendar but ever new in their interpretation. He preached several times a day.

Romero was not happy living in emergency mode. As he noted after an exhausting attempt at mediation—to convince a political organization to stop occupying the French Embassy and to release some hostages—he was very glad to return to his usual religious activities:

> That afternoon [I] took a much-needed, long rest from pastoral work by accepting Father Cayo Ayala's invitation to go to San José Villanueva, his hometown, to celebrate the sixtieth wedding anniversary of Father Ayala's parents. It coincided with the end of the month of May. And at the local church, May flowers had been brought by the different sectors of the parish that were under the care of the Passionist sisters. [It was] a beautiful moment for a pastoral afternoon to talk about the Blessed Mother, the sanctity of marriage and fidelity, the gift of life, and of holy fruitfulness. These are topics for a simple atmosphere. There were also many children who had come from school; it seemed like the whole school was there. Giving a talk in simple, pastoral language and greeting the people as they departed [by] shaking their hands, leaves upon the soul a mark of serenity and a sense of being rooted in love with a people that know how to reciprocate.

Romero adopted as his own the Second Vatican Council's preferential option for the poor, a teaching which was then repeated in Medellín. He was moved to see the "good faith of the humble people." This did not imply any dislike of the rich. Romero believed, according to the classical thought of the Church, that the rich had greater difficulties in saving their souls, and that salvation was by way of generosity, giving, charity to the poor. According to Romero, the rich were condemned by selfishness and avarice, not wealth itself. "It is not that those who have many possessions are condemned, but they must become humble, poor, needy of God, if they want to find forgiveness and the grace of salvation." Wealth was not necessarily negative but should not give rise to illusions: "Look brethren, worldly fame, power, money, the glory of the world, are good for nothing. Really, nothing! They all end with death." Romero insisted on sharing and distributing riches. He spoke of the risk that wealthy people ran with their "idolatrous worship of their wealth," but he did not discriminate against them. When violence claimed victims, Romero extended his condolences, making no distinction between rich and poor, between the dead on one side or on the other. No one was excluded from Christian piety, policemen and peasants, soldiers and guerrilla fighters, oligarchs and laborers: "I still believe what I said at the funerals of the engineer Borgonovo and Father Navarro: every life is sacred, whether of a rich man or of a poor man."

Romero's archdiocese was pluralistic in allowing many movements and expressions of the faith. Romero had personal ties with the Christian Cursillos and with Opus Dei; he made friendly visits to Alcoholics Anonymous; he had good relations with the Neocatechumenal Movement and the Knights of Christ the King, with Marriage Encounter groups and the charismatics; he promoted Marian devotion and the worship of the Sacred Heart; he was actively involved in Cáritas El Salvador. He believed that a movement had to respect three criteria in order to be truly ecclesial: adherence to the Gospel; approval by the Church; love for the poor. He remarked: "The danger of any movement lies in going to extremes: either too much activity or too much spiritualism. There must be a balance between prayer and work for one's neighbor."

As archbishop, Romero understood better than before how the poverty of his people resulted from social injustice. However, he did not set aside his practice of individual charity. He used to send alms to the poor who wrote to him. He signed letters of recommendation for those seeking work, to introduce people, and to help needy families. He resided at Divine Providence Hospital for poor, terminally ill patients, and he visited them every month. For Romero, the demand for structural reform was not an alternative to direct aid to the poor. Along with the need for basic social and political solutions, the need for personal compassion also remained.

The theme of poverty reminded Romero of the theme of holiness:

> The center of my life is to witness to God's love for humanity and to the love of human beings for one another. This must be manifested through our own lives and conduct as Christians, with a living witness of fidelity to Jesus Christ, of poverty and detachment from material goods, and of freedom from the powers of the world. In a word: sanctity.

As archbishop, Romero did not aspire to holiness as a beginner would, in terms of mortification, imitation of exemplary figures, or constant vigilance against temptations. In his spiritual life he was no longer a novice. Now he turned to Christ, to his passion and cross. Against the background of his life, he glimpsed the possibility of martyrdom as the highest form of union with Christ. Now he emphasized mission more than virtues: "In my capacity as a pastor, I think that I must carry out the mission of purifying the history of our people, both from the sin of injustice and from the violation of the rights of the poor. Christ is already walking with us on this journey, and he wants us to reach the fullness of history, after having cultivated his love and his peace in the justice of his Gospel."

The Preacher

In preaching, Romero felt that he was fulfilling his role as a bishop. The cathedral (or the church that substituted for it due to frequent occupations) was the primary place of Romero's activity. At the altar, Romero seemed to be transformed. He gained self-assurance and preached with power and authority. His words had magnetism: people listened to him for hours without their attention flagging. When he finished speaking, however, he was exhausted.

In his preaching Romero was easy to understand and struck a familiar tone. Although the homilies were given at eight in the morning in order to avoid the tropical heat of the day, they seemed more like evening fireside chats with close friends. Besides commenting at length on the daily Scripture readings, Romero would speak about his meetings, news about the Church and the nation, or his experiences that week. He would also report information that he gathered from the diocesan offices and from the Church's grassroots network in the countryside. He took few political or diplomatic precautions. Many described Romero's homilies with one word: "*Verdad.*" He could establish a special personal, intimate relationship with his listeners, even though his tone was never complacent, captivating, or casual. Instead he had the lofty and solemn tone of an orator, which indeed he was. Moreover Romero spoke about nothing less than God. For example in his homily on March 9, 1980, he said:

> When God says [to Moses]: "I am who am; I am being," he means: I am the dynamic presence; I am the one who must be discovered in the dynamism of history. I am present in the workings of all the powers of the world. I am the force of the stars and

of the seas. I am the one who makes things exist. Therefore he also tells him: "I am the God of Abraham, the God of Isaac, the God of Jacob." Do not have an abstract idea of me, a God who is up in heaven and has left earth to people; that is not right. The God of heaven is the God of earth. He is the God who is building history, who walks with the patriarchs, who walks with fathers of families. He is the God of my ancestors, the God of the whole task of my homeland.... He is a God who wants to be with humanity, a God who feels the pain of someone who is tortured and killed, a God who condemns with the Church, who denounces torture, repression, and all such crimes. The God whom we adore is not a dead God. He is a living God who hears, acts, works, and guides this history, and in him we hope, in him we trust.

The faithful looked forward to hearing Romero's words. The term *homilía* became part of the common vocabulary of Salvadorans. His preaching was either listened to and revered, or rejected with disgust. According to Romero himself, it suffered the fate of all Christian preaching: "Some accept it and are happy, others reject it and persist in their wickedness." Romero denounced injustices, violations of human dignity, and the tragic events in the country. He was unyielding in his defense of the victims of tyranny and in his affirmation of the rights of the poor. But this did not make his preaching political. An expression that often occurs in Romero's homilies summarizes their foundation: "*Primero Dios*—God first." God first established the natural law, which we must not violate by sin, oppression, and violence.

In his homilies, Romero closely correlated biblical commentary with human history: "We are not talking about the stars," he used to say. The tendency to make his preaching relevant did not rule out classical language. Romero referred to "being brave soldiers of Christ the King." He insisted on virtues like magnanimity. He used descriptive adjectives like *adamant* and *inviolable*. At the same time he spoke in a lively, clear way that was never pompous. If he had to discuss the martyrdom of Saint Bartholomew, he would not avoid saying that the apostle had been "skinned alive." If the Salvadoran press maintained a "conspiracy of silence" on important events, whereas the international press made them front-page news, he would exclaim: "What cripples we are!" In Romero's homilies we come across passages like the following:

> The word is like a ray of sunlight that comes from above and illumines. Is it the sun's fault when its most pure light encounters puddles, dung, and dirt on this earth? It has to illuminate these things. Otherwise it would not be sunlight; it would not be light; it would not uncover the ugly, horrible things that exist on earth.
>
> Independence Month sounds like a sarcastic joke in these hours of so much slavery. . . . The Scripture readings have a sad image of slavery: the desert. The desert! They say that when the Bedouins cross the desert, they hear the noise of the wind from far away. Being imaginative, they say: "Do you hear how the wind sounds? It is the desert lamenting and weeping because it would like to be a garden!" I think there is no more eloquent image of man's need than the image of the thirsty desert, an immense, sterile expanse of sand. An image of the true need for independence, for advancement.
>
> How sad it is to read that in El Salvador the two leading causes of death are, first, diarrhea, and second, right after it, murder, when people die by homicide or as a result of their injuries. These are the statistics. So that right after the sign of malnutrition, diarrhea, there is the sign of crime, murder. These two epidemics are killing our people.

Romero's homilies had no ambiguities that needed interpretation: the language was very clear. The lucidity of thought was accompanied by a strong passion and appeal to the emotions. This was the extraordinary mix of Romero's preaching, which was serious and solemn yet not formal. Sometimes, by the intimate tone with which he addressed the faithful in the cathedral and the nation listening on the radio, Romero seemed to be conversing with a few friends. Frankness, candor, and trust shone through his preaching. This disconcerted the cunning and the skeptics but won over the people to his way of thinking.

Romero's fluent oratory allowed him to improvise on any subject, but the basic guidelines were not improvised. Indeed, Romero was deliberately repetitive. For him, a homily was an explanation of the Scripture readings, an exhortation, and an oft-repeated invitation to faith and conversion. The connection with the magisterium of the Church was a recurring feature in all of Romero's preaching. He never failed to quote from the popes and the Second Vatican Council. In about two hundred published homilies, Romero cites Paul VI and John Paul II 373 times, Vatican II 296 times, Puebla 101 times, and Medellín 85 times, not to mention the less frequent citations of the teachings of other Popes, from Leo XIII to Pius XI. In 1979 and 1980 the quotations from John Paul II and Puebla are especially frequent. Romero's favorite magisterial documents were *Gaudium et Spes* and *Evangelii Nuntiandi*.

Romero's preaching focuses on several central themes: sin, penance, conversion, forgiveness. Romero mentioned them not in the abstract but in relation to the current situation of his country: violence from various sources, social injustice, kidnappings and the disappearance of persons, repression and terrorist attacks. For Romero, the heart of the biblical proclamation was the transition from evil to good, exemplified in the death and resurrection of Christ. Thus he preached in May 1977, having in mind the assassination of Father Navarro, which had occurred a few days earlier:

> Christ began to preach the Good News with a penitential word, and it is the essence of the Church's preaching: "Repent, convert,

leave the paths of wickedness." How appropriate it is to go out in this hour into all the streets of the country, where we find so much hatred, so much calumny, so much revenge, so much perversity of heart, and to say: "Convert." If the Church rejects violence, if the Church will never approve of crimes such as those that were committed this week, she does not do it with hatred toward the one who fired the gun, who killed, who kidnapped. But she says to him with love: "Convert." . . . The Blessed Virgin asks us this evening: "Convert." Conversion also from the sins that everyone carries in his heart. I too carry my own sins, and so does each one of you. Which one of us here is not a sinner? Let us ask forgiveness of the Lord; let us convert; let us abandon the path of wickedness.

Romero was convinced that the only real solution to the problems troubling the country was a religious solution. A general conversion was needed, of the poor and of the rich, of the ruling class and of the *campesinos*. This conversion had to be personal, however, because the sin was personal:

> The prophet Ezekiel says that when sin exists, each one is responsible in God's sight for his own conscience. Let us not forget this, brothers and sisters. Certainly the bishops in Medellín said that there is such a thing as structural sin, a communal, social sin; this is what we call the surroundings. But despite the surroundings, despite the structures of sin, God will not call the structures to account. He will call to account every man and woman who lives in those structures. God's judgment, says the prophet Ezekiel, will be according to each one's actions. If an evil man has converted and now does what is right and practices justice, he will live. God will save him because he has converted. And if a good man, however holy he may be, becomes perverted and does the deeds of the wicked, because of his deeds he will be lost; he will die.

In order to convert, it is necessary to repent and to experience forgiveness. This is the noblest thing that could happen among persons: "What a very beautiful thing is the forgiveness of sins. . . . It is like turning a desert into a garden." Romero insisted on the need for forgiveness. In his personal life, he sought to set an example of the practice of forgiveness. In every tragic circumstance, Romero spoke words of forgiveness. He asked forgiveness for murderers, for the violent, for sinners, even exclaiming: "The vengeance of God is forgiveness!" Forgiveness calms minds and reconciles after a tragedy, whenever the guilty ones were willing to repent. During Navarro's funeral, Romero emphasized the message of forgiveness:

> A priest, riddled with bullets, who dies forgiving, who dies praying, speaks his message to all of us gathered around his grave. . . . I wish to give thanks for the witness of the good woman who held him as he was in agony, bleeding, who asked him what hurt, and he told her: "What hurts me the most is the pardon that I would like to give to my assassins, to those who shot me, and the sorrow that I feel for my sins. May the Lord forgive me." And he began to pray. That is how those who believe in God die, even with their human weaknesses and their sins. . . . This is the message of Alfonso Navarro: . . . "Not this way, not through the vain illusion of hatred, not through the philosophy of an eye for an eye and a tooth for a tooth, which is criminal," but by this other path: "Love one another."

Romero in Private

In public, Romero showed firmness and mastery of topics. In private, he was not the same way. Romero sought advice, was vulnerable, asked for forgiveness, and dialogued in order to understand. He was willing to meet with anybody, friends and adversaries, rebels and military men, rich and poor. On the one hand, Romero was conscious of his national role, and on the other hand, Romero was in search of humanity, truth, and solutions. Those were turbulent years. Archbishop Romero sadly said that it was his "destiny to go gathering corpses." Romero was astounded by the "density" of "our history": "In a short time many events and changes can happen." There was much confusion. In the words of Rivera Damas: "*Monseñor* Romero happened to be pastor of the archdiocese in very difficult and terribly confusing historical times." Romero compared El Salvador to Jerusalem where the three wise men arrived, confused because they no longer could see the guiding star and were forced into a "humble search":

> No one should pretend to know everything. The Magi arrived in Jerusalem and then became confused. They even felt the need to go ask Herod. And Herod did not know either; he had to consult the interpreters of the Bible. No one owns the truth, only God. And someone who wants to walk in the truth must be humble and seek the truth along with others. I don't go to a dialogue in order to impose my way of thinking. You go to dialogue to find out the other's response, what I lack: it is a search. . . . It is worth the trouble, especially when what is sought is something so great as the good of the country.

Even the administration of the archdiocese did not escape the surrounding emergencies and confusion. On some days it was difficult for Romero to welcome visitors without being constantly interrupted by urgent messages or telephone calls. If he trusted the guest, he would then invite him to talk in peace in his car. In Romero's curia, assignments easily passed from person to person. Councils, committees, departments, and secretariats vied for competencies and responsibilities, competing with an invasive, ideological, political environment that was ceaselessly calling for public statements.

Certain sectors of the curia pressured for greater political involvement by Romero and the diocese in support of leftist organizations. These sectors were mainly the Peace and Justice Commission, the Secretariat for Human Rights, Legal Aid, and the Office for the Pastoral Care of Workers and Labor. Occasionally, for short periods, the revolutionary movement even used the seminary, because some seminarians wanted it. Eventually Romero indefinitely suspended the Commission for the Laity because of its excessive independence from the diocese. Its leaders were also politically involved, militantly supporting the popular organizations.

The diocesan media were a trouble spot in Romero's Church. Their management was criticized by *La Nacional*, the base communities, and politicized Catholics. Requests were made to increase the radio station's commitment to "consciousness raising," not to run commercials or "romantic-bourgeois" songs, and to get over its "excess of human prudence." Some complained that the diocesan press should dedicate more space to the defense of priests and faithful affected by the repression, and to "become incarnate in the deeds of the people" and "not to extinguish the spirit of prophecy." The Church was "the people," and therefore the Catholic media too had to be "of the people." Instead, those in charge of the diocesan media (the newspaper *Orientación* and Radio YSAX), on orders from Romero, tried to control what was published or aired, so that the Church would not be reduced to a political entity.

Romero's closest associates—Bishop Rivera Damas, while he remained in San Salvador; the vicar general Ricardo Urioste; the rector of the seminary, Gregorio Rosa Chávez; media director Doris Osegueda; and secretary Jesús Delgado—shared the archbishop's religious views and his ideas about Salvadoran society. They defended him when he was attacked or slandered. Basing themselves on the documents of Vatican II, Medellín, and Puebla, they were convinced that the Church should implement a preferential option for the poor and that the country had to be reformed for the sake of justice. They did not like extremism and did not want the Church to be subordinate to the demands of politics. The option for the poor was not political in itself but religious, connected to the recent magisterium of the Church.

Romero used to go from meeting to meeting. He authorized the various work teams to intervene on behalf of the archdiocese, although he sometimes disavowed their work with a personal change of opinion. He confessed to himself: "I have to correct my excessive speed in making decisions that I later reverse." He was not a good staff coordinator. He felt at ease in the pulpit, preaching, making pastoral visits, especially in the most humble environments. He was a pastor, not an administrator. He noted in February, 1980: "Administration: my neglect, careful! Personnel. Respect coworkers. Avoid disorderliness." Romero was more adept in caring for souls than in organizing the diocese. As archbishop, Romero went from intense spiritual conversations in private, to the prophetic words of a great preacher. Structuring the curia, running meetings, and coordinating efforts were not among his strong points. Impulsive as he was, Romero, unlike his predecessor Chávez, could offer his personal trust at one moment only to withdraw it in the next. Living in a constant state of emergency, beset by all kinds of requests, and subject to continuous pressures that prevented him from keeping a regular schedule, Romero did not have the time to gain an in-depth understanding of his collaborators, about whom he often had doubts. In a sense, Romero maintained little space between the two opposite poles of friend and enemy. At times he could be infuriated with someone, but he would immediately examine his actions. If he thought that he was at fault, he would ask forgiveness right away, as he had done in the years before he was appointed archbishop. Some collaborators, however, constantly enjoyed his esteem. Besides Rivera Damas, whom Romero considered "his best friend," these included the priests Delgado, Rosa, Urioste, and Amaya, whom he repeatedly proposed as candidates for vacant episcopal sees. In the last year of his life, Romero worked closely with a young priest, Rafael Urrutia. The latter gave the following portrait of Romero, torn between contemplative prayer and the urgency of acting: "He was a man unlike any other. He was shy, simple, intelligent, nervous, even irascible, but then he was ready to ask forgiveness for his temper. For him everything was urgent, everything had to be done immediately. But above all, he was a man of prayer."

In private, Romero was methodical and precise. He packed his own bags with meticulous care. If he had time he would exercise in his room. He enjoyed taking strolls and loved to walk and move about. He was interested in everything and was as curious as a child. When he travelled to places where he was not known, he liked to visit markets, look at the people, watch children playing, and talk to everybody. He was a simple man, happy if he could stay with other simple people, eating simple meals and perhaps drinking a few sips of whiskey with friends who enjoyed that. He loved the movies and the circus like a child would. He would go to a cinema whenever he was away from El Salvador.

His residence at Divine Providence Hospital consisted of a modest apartment that had been designed for a watchman. It had three small rooms with basic furniture and no hint of luxury. It was by the road, on the edge of the campus of the hospital, which treated the terminally ill. In his early days as archbishop he didn't even have his own house. He used to sleep on a cot in the sacristy of the hospital chapel. Upon taking possession of the archdiocese, he had declined the offer of a large, comfortable house in one of the affluent neighborhoods of San Salvador. The offer had been made by families belonging to the oligarchy. He thought that the Church of Vatican II had to be poor, without luxuries for its ministers. However he did not decline the attentive care of the nuns who ran the small hospital or of the youngest daughter of his friend Barraza. The following excerpt is from Barraza himself, describing one of the many Sundays in which Romero was his guest:

> [After the liturgy] we went to my house. You could tell that Romero felt quite content but very tired. As usual, when he arrived, he took off his heavier clothes and remained lightly clad in pants and a shirt. As was his custom, he leaned back in an easy chair to watch the cartoons on television. He took off his shoes and put on slippers. As on every Sunday we offered him a little aperitif, usually a shot of whisky, which soothed his throat. Then he watched television like a child, playing with Chavo and Virginia, while Lupe and I sat on the floor. These were brief moments in which to play like children. Someone would take away his cushion, he would distractedly tug at the hair of one of the children, and another child would sneak up to tickle him. We all enjoyed ourselves . . . "Food's on the table." Occasionally he fell asleep in front of the television, after taking one or two sips of the aperitif. Obviously, after the demanding Sunday homily and all that nervous tension, he felt relieved of a great weight. Then, too, on Saturday night he often stayed awake until the first light of dawn, preparing his homily.

With Journalists

Archbishop Romero quickly rose to great international fame, due to the crucial efforts of journalists. Romero was constantly in the spotlight, in the press and on television. In the late 1970s El Salvador was a crucial country in the recovery from the Cold War

between East and West. It became the scene of a violent and ideological confrontation that fired up the media. Romero appeared in
the center of this clash. He was like a new David, armed only with
his words in the fight against the Goliath of a brutal military government. *Time* depicted Romero as "the most outspoken bishop in
Latin America" in terms of human rights, titling an article about
him "An Archbishop Without Fear." On the part of the media, this
wasn't a fabrication but something of a stretch. It sought to depict
Romero from a political perspective as an opposition leader. Romero
noticed the repetitiveness of the interviews and of the topics discussed in them. This resulted in an authentic but incomplete portrait
of a human rights hero. His thoughts were often presented selec-
tively, excluding the religious aspect. The Romero of the press was a
radical figure, unbalanced in his politics. That was quite different
from the real Romero, who was certainly audacious but also
moderate.

Romero was happy to be in such demand and to be interviewed
by the international press. After the Sunday liturgy in the cathedral,
he usually held a press conference, in which groups of correspondents participated. The archbishop did not avoid journalists,
maintaining that this too was "work to spread the kingdom of God
on earth." Romero knew that the media might manipulate his
words. He sometimes noted that newspapers attributed to him
things he had never said. Even after his death, Romero was often
presented not so much in the context of his whole message, but on
the basis of phrases intended for effect, which could be called slogans. One of Romero's expressions in particular is universally
known: *"Si me matan, resucitaré en el pueblo salvadoreño."* "If they
kill me, I will rise again in the people of El Salvador." The authenticity of this phrase, incessantly repeated in books and articles on
Romero, rests on the good faith of a Guatemalan journalist from the

Mexican newspaper *Excelsior,* José Calderón Salazar. He claims to have heard it from Romero during a telephone conversation two weeks before he was killed. Calderón made it known only after the archbishop's death, by publishing a text that immediately became famous as though it were the murdered man's last will and testament. Here it is in full:

> I have often been threatened with death. But I must say that as a Christian, I do not believe in death without resurrection. If they kill me I will rise again in the people of El Salvador. I say this without any boasting; I say it with great humility. As a pastor I am obligated by a divine command to give my life for those whom I love. That means all Salvadorans, even those who are going to kill me. If they do indeed carry out their threats, from this moment I offer my blood for the redemption and resurrection of El Salvador. Martyrdom is a grace of God that I don't think I deserve. But if God accepts the sacrifice of my life, may my blood be a seed of liberty and a sign that hope will soon become a reality. If God accepts my death, may it be for my people's freedom and a witness of hope. You may say, if they succeed in killing me, that I forgive and bless the perpetrators. Hopefully they will realize it would only be a waste of their time. A bishop will die, but God's Church, which is the people, will never perish.

This text stands at the center of the myth of Romero as a populist political prophet. It was published in *Excelsior* on March 25, 1980, next to the news of Romero's assassination. It was immediately picked up by the major international news agencies and had great success. On March 26, 1980, many newspapers were already presenting the figure of Romero based on the words attributed to him by the Guatemalan journalist. Many of Romero's collaborators, however, expressed puzzlement about Calderón's article. The suspicion that it was apocryphal was suggested above all by the remark, *"Si me matan, resucitaré en el pueblo salvadoreño."* Rivera Damas thought that that sentence was at the very least inaccurately reported. Rosa Chávez has always doubted its authenticity.

The alleged telephone call from Calderón is not verified in the primary or secondary sources about Romero. It has incorrect chronological references to Romero's calendar. It must be emphasized that Calderón's article dated March 25, 1980, is posthumous with respect to Romero. Calderón had never previously quoted any of those compelling, thunderous remarks by the archbishop, assuming that he had ever heard, memorized, and noted them. Calderón did not put these words into Romero's mouth until shortly after his death, when the archbishop was no longer able to refute or correct anything. Furthermore, too many bombastic expressions are used to create an effect. As anxious as the Guatemalan journalist is to stress the confidential nature of the interview, the published text does not seem typical of a telephone conversation, of the kind that Romero could have had with a person who was not only distant but also probably unknown to him. As a matter of fact, Calderón did not cover news about Romero or even El Salvador regularly (*Excelsior* had other correspondents in San Salvador and its stories about Salvadoran issues usually appeared with other bylines).

In all the sources about Romero we find no expressions like those attributed to him by Calderón. In particular, there is nothing analogous to the statement, *"Si me matan, resucitaré en el pueblo salvadoreño."* In fact, other source materials contain expressions that mean the opposite. During his last spiritual retreat, two weeks before the alleged telephone call with Calderón, Romero wrote that he did not want to assign to his likely death any specific "intention," whether religious or civic. He added: "the Heart of Christ will know how to take things to their desired destiny." On the subject of his own possible death, Romero's tones are always subdued, quite different from those reported by Calderón. In his last months, Romero had a clear perception of the danger of death, but he would not waste time talking about it.

The words that Romero spoke about his own death (according to Calderón) seem to echo not so much the archbishop's usual thoughts but the barrage of slogans used by popular political organizations in reaction to his murder. On that same evening of March 24, 1980, while Calderón composed his original obituary, graffiti such as these appeared on the walls of El Salvador: *"¡Monseñor Romero no ha muerto; vive en el corazón de todo un pueblo que lucha incansablemente!"* [2] or *"¡Monseñor Romero vive en el corazón y las luchas del pueblo!"* [3]

Two years earlier, Calderón had been threatened with death in Guatemala. He had published a sort of celebratory poem for his own death and resurrection, in terms similar to those he would publish about Romero on March 25, 1980. This makes the hypothesis that the words attributed by Calderón to the martyred archbishop were apocryphal all the more probable.

A Man Much in Demand

The Peers of England proposed Romero for the Nobel Prize. The President of the United States, Jimmy Carter, began to take note of his appeals. This resulted from the work of the media, but Romero would not have attracted journalists if he hadn't had the

---

2. "Archbishop Romero has not died; he lives in the heart of those who struggle untiringly!" —*Trans.*

3. "Archbishop Romero lives in the heart and in the struggles of the people!" —*Trans.*

prestige derived from his courageous preaching, his trust in the power of good, and his love for the poor. On every side, many people—politicians, priests, journalists, soldiers, guerrilla fighters, intellectuals, people from every walk of life—sought to have Romero on their side. They flattered him and made a show of having his consensus, support, and guidance.

The Jesuits of El Salvador were accused of having influenced Romero. There is nothing wrong with trying to influence someone, to persuade him of one's own convictions, to convey one's own ideas to him. All human relations contain in some way the seed of mutual influence. It is the normal course of life. The Salvadoran Jesuits unabashedly admitted their attempt to influence Romero, while adding that his superiority in the relationship with them was clear. Similarly, many others tried to influence Romero, to orient him, to win him over. Did Romero let anyone influence him? We might think so, given his stance in favor of the Revolutionary Junta which on October 15, 1979, overthrew the government of General Romero on the basis of a program of social reforms. For some months, Romero became unpopular with the politicized sectors of the Church. Priests from *La Nacional* and base communities criticized him. The Archbishop's chancery was occupied by a leftist organization, thanks to the complicity of some priests. Romero received death threats from the left. Yet Romero was free from ideological dogmatism. He thought, rightly or wrongly, that the new government could spare El Salvador a civil war, and so he gave them a conditional vote of confidence.

Undoubtedly, Romero did not act alone but made concerted efforts with his collaborators. Yet as Rivera Damas noted: "He was resolute. He would listen to everybody, but then he would make up his own mind." When Romero had to write demanding documents, he would ask for help from co-workers and experts. His third pastoral letter was reviewed by at least twenty-five people before its release. Romero liked to compare different opinions, but the final version was his own work. He often completely ignored the suggestions of others. Considering his high office, it would have been unwise for him not to use the competent staff that he had available in the diocese, although he would always write the final draft.

Romero followed a practice of moral theology to which he had always been faithful in doubtful matters. He would make his decision after collecting different, sometimes conflicting opinions. Romero spoke with a wide variety of people, and even his friendships did not conform to predetermined plans. As archbishop, he organized his spiritual direction in a complex way. His confessor was an elderly Jesuit, Father Azcue, an old-fashioned priest, considered in the diocese to be a "sacramentalist." Yet Azcue believed in the preferential option for the poor. At the same time, Romero had a spiritual guide in Father Sáenz Lacalle, an Opus Dei priest with whom he kept in contact even as archbishop. He accepted Sáenz's invitation to attend a monthly day of reflection and fellowship with the priests of Opus Dei. On the day of his death, too, Romero participated in a fraternal meeting of priests organized by Opus Dei, which, on that twenty-fourth of March, was combined with a trip to the beach. As though Azcue and Sáenz were not enough, occasionally Romero addressed spiritual issues that preoccupied him with the Redemptorist Fermín Aranguren, whose approach was rather traditional. Romero conferred with these three priests, receiving opinions that did not always agree with his own. That was what he wanted. Romero knew that life is not an exercise in logic but is rather made up of polarities that often coexist.

When he had to make decisions, however, Romero could not reconcile differences beyond a certain limit. For this reason, he made his most delicate choices only after praying before the Blessed

Sacrament. He did so each time a disagreement occurred and he was not sure of his judgment. After listening, he would withdraw to pray. He would then return to a meeting, sometimes shifting the orientation of the debate or simply cutting it short.

Romero sensed that many were trying to influence him, and he feared that he would not notice it: "I fear the ideological and political influences. I can be influenced and imprudent decisions can occur." Such awareness, though, was the best guarantee of freedom. Romero was pressured from every side, with flattery from the left and threats from the right. All the factions had understood the archbishop's importance in national politics.

Many people boasted of their friendship with the archbishop without good reason. Romero was indulgent. He used to say: "It is likely that they are using me; I ask God that they may use me for good ends." He needed consensus, both domestic and international, in order to bear the brunt of the persecution of his local church and to demand justice in the country. The Salvadoran press, owned by families of the oligarchy that considered him a dangerous subversive, opposed and slandered him. He was opposed by Molina's government and then by the regime of General Romero, who shared the same last name.

Romero was indeed a "man much in demand," as Jean Meyer described him, a man whom everybody sought. He was under pressure, overwhelmed not only by his schedule but also by many who called on him with their needs and urgent concerns, often without prior notice. All the current issues and problems of the nation ended up on Romero's desk. He belonged to everyone, welcomed everyone, answered everyone. In all this, he used a method: to dialogue with everyone, which was not easy in a polarized situation where the two opposing factions saw betrayal if one so much as listened to the opponent. In a country torn by the most brutal violence, dialogue was not easy at all. Salvadoran politics knew no compromise or mediation. It was not soft politics according to the rules of fair play, but politics driven by machismo and the desire to annihilate the opponent. Romero was perhaps the only one in El Salvador at a high level who could communicate with both sides in the conflict. He was authoritative not because of his political abilities but because of his personal reputation. Romero knew and quoted the words of Pius XI: "Dialogue is the way to many solutions. If it were for the good of the Church, I would dialogue with the devil himself."[4] Romero commented: "To dialogue is not to empathize, nor to be an accomplice. But it can happen that, if we listen, we may find justice even in what is 'illegal.' "

The image of a Romero unwilling to dialogue with the powerful has been cultivated by opposing political sides, on the one hand to praise Romero's allegedly anti-government stance, or on the other hand to censure his supposed political maximalism. Romero did not want his presence at public ceremonies to be seen as a tacit approval of the evil done by a government that gave free rein to repressive forces that killed and tortured. But he made himself available to talk privately with presidents and ministers, if they wished, just as he courteously received members of the oligarchy and of the business world. Repeatedly he sent his representatives to discuss and seek solutions with the civilian authorities. The archdiocese participated in round table meetings organized by the government and the

---

4. This quotation from Pius XI seems to be derived from a talk he gave on May 14, 1929, at the College of Mondragone: *"Quando si trattasse di salvare qualche anima, di impedire maggiori danni di anime, ci sentiremmo il coraggio di trattare col diavolo in persona."* "When it is a question of saving souls, or preventing greater harm to souls, we feel the courage to deal with the devil in person." —*Ed.*

Church, some of which came about thanks to efforts made in Rome by Agostino Casaroli. At the same time Romero also had to admit that other groups were not very willing to dialogue, because any negotiation concerning the state of the country was viewed as a prop in political theater and not as an effort to seriously address problems. Romero was not interested in chatting with the country's leaders. He felt the urgent need to resolve the situations that he considered tragic. He was anxious to get news about the *desaparecidos*, those who had "disappeared" at the hands of security forces, but also to free the hostages held by the guerrillas. For this reason, on the one hand he talked with the President of the Republic, and on the other hand he agreed to go blindfolded to guerrilla headquarters.

The method of dialogue presupposed a goal, one that Romero had clearly in mind. It was to end the violence, and to do this through social justice. The crisis would be overcome if the ruling class took into account the need to remedy the injustice that was so widespread in society, and if the opposition acted responsibly. Romero did not weigh how realistic his campaign was. He radiated hope precisely because he did not calculate his chances of success. He thought that his actions were realistic by the measure of faith, not reason. Recalling a meeting with Romero, Maurizio Chierici alludes to this:

> February 1980. It was a bad time. Because the cathedral was occupied, Mass was not celebrated there, but in another church, Sacred Heart, I think. There was the left-wing underground; the guerrilla war did not let up. They did not accept words of peace. Attempts at dialogue failed, and the right-wing military was unleashed. *Monseñor* Romero was also very distressed because of the wave of refugees who arrived in the capital. . . . But at the end of that meeting, he was very optimistic. He said: "I will get the military to agree, including those who do not agree, and then I will get the guerrillas to agree too. Some guerrilla fighters are

ready for dialogue and negotiations, and I think that I can make peace." We asked him how he could get them all to agree in a situation of death, violence, repression, hunger, and fear. Wasn't that merely a utopia? Smiling, he looked at us and replied: "Excuse me, if I did not believe in utopia, would I go around dressed like this?"

Romero and Liberation Theology

Liberation theologians presented Romero's activity as the embodiment of that theology, although he was not a follower of it. For his part, Romero was concerned about following the official theology of the Church. He did not feel that he was a professional theologian. His reading focused on the documents of the magisterium, patristic texts, biblical commentaries, and lives of the saints, and it was usually related to his preaching. He devoted much more time to prayer than to scholarly reading. He liked to read books by Eduardo Pironio, who echoed themes from liberation theology in his typical pastoral, religious, mystical, non-political style. Through Pironio he became acquainted with a formulation of liberation theology that he considered reliably faithful to the Gospel and the magisterium of the Church. In 1978, Romero wrote to the Argentine Cardinal: "Your *Estudios Pastorales* are, in my opinion, tremendously relevant. I have used them as an authentic evangelical inspiration in my sincere desire to implement the guidelines from Medellín."

If Romero was interested in understanding what liberation theology proclaimed, it was for pastoral reasons, since some of his priests sympathetically followed that theology. It was also out of a sort of Latin American patriotism that made him look benevolently at all that was produced locally, in the field of spirituality too. It was his respect for "the theology that is developing on our continent," as he wrote to an Italian publisher in 1979. Romero sensed the problem of the identity of the continental Church. In March 1979, John Paul II approved the *Documento de Puebla* as a contribution to the "specific identity" of the Latin American Church. According to Romero, the Pope's expression was as if to say:

> You have a very Latin American way, you are very special, your Church has a way of being that is not the same as the Church of Europe, or of Africa, or of any other place. Seek to discover more and more this Latin American identity of your Church and live it with its problems, needs, and challenges.

Moreover, Romero told his collaborators that it was unnecessary to resort to theological insights just for the sake of novelty or liberation, but to work in accordance with the Gospel Beatitudes. He reasoned precisely as a pastor and not as a theologian. Certainly Romero spoke about the sin that had crept into societal structures, recalling a theme of liberation theology, but he also he spoke about individual sin. He knew the people's daily life with its miseries, troubles, and frailties. Real redemption was found in conversion:

> When we preach the Word of the Lord, we not only denounce the injustices of the social order, we denounce every sin that is night and shadow: drunkenness, gluttony, lust, adultery, abortion, all that which belongs to the reign of iniquity and sin. . . . Only by walking along paths of light, honesty and sanctity; interiorly clothing ourselves with Christ; being converted even though we have been a sinner, but being converted to the Lord; only in this way, will we be able to walk toward the goal and truly build peace.

The day before he was killed, he said:

> How easy it is to denounce structural injustice, institutionalized violence, social sin! All this is certainly true, but where are the

wellsprings of this social sin? In the heart of every human being. Present-day society is like a sort of anonymous society in which nobody wants to take responsibility and all are responsible. . . . We are all sinners and we all have added our grain of sand to this mountain of crimes and violence in our country. Therefore, salvation starts with man, with the dignity of the human being, with rooting out sin from every individual. And in Lent, this is God's call: Convert individually! Among all those present, no two sinners are alike. Each one has committed his own shameless deeds, yet we want to blame others and hide our own. I need to take off the mask, for I too am one of these. I must ask God for forgiveness because I have offended God and society.

Romero had more faith in new persons than in new structures:

[In Lent] we do not mortify ourselves out of an unhealthy desire to suffer. God did not make us for suffering. If there are fasts, if there are penances, if there is prayer, it is because we have a very positive goal, which a human being reaches by overcoming himself: Easter, or the Resurrection. So we not only celebrate a Christ who rises in a way different from ours, but during Lent we can gain the ability to rise with him to a new life, to become those new men and women who are needed in this country, especially today. Let us not just shout slogans about changing structures, because new structures have no use when there are no new human beings to manage and live in them.

In the Catholicism of Romero's time, progressives emphasized social sin, and conservatives emphasized individual sin. According to Romero, evil permeated both persons and society. Unjust structures existed because of the sin of individuals. Sin had individual roots, but it was also widespread in society. Romero called persons to conversion first of all: "The root of the evils in today's world is inside the person; the remedy must start from the heart." Romero recognized that evil was capable of taking material form in history and could be perceived in society beyond individual persons. Yet it had to be fought in the first place with a personal examination of conscience: "Christ crucified is preaching to me personally. Before speaking and criticizing others, I have to look to myself, because I too have nailed Christ to the cross with my sins." Romero felt no contradiction in denouncing both personal sin and structural sin.

Romero was convinced of the centrality of the poor in Christianity. He did not need, therefore, to quote liberation theologians. He cited Paul VI, John Paul II, Vatican II, Medellín, Puebla. He explained the Beatitudes in this way:

> The great goods that a Christian hopes for must not be what is hoped for by the people whom we call prestigious: to have more politically, socially, and economically. This is not what interests a Christian. . . . For me Christ is wisdom, justice, sanctification, redemption. What more do I want? . . . This is the heart's treasure of someone who is poor and humble, who does not base his happiness on transitory things—which you cannot take with you when you die, which are carried away by time—but on what is lasting, such as the wisdom of Christ, his justice, his sanctification, his redemption. Blessed are the poor! Because they know where their treasure is, in him who, although he was rich, made himself poor so as to enrich us by his poverty, to teach us the true wisdom of the Christian. . . . Some young people do not believe that a better world can be made by the love of the Beatitudes, but instead choose violence, guerrilla warfare, revolution. The Church will never make this path her own; once again this is quite clear. . . . The Church's choice is this page from Christ's Gospel: the Beatitudes. I tell you, I am not surprised that it is not understood. . . . The world does not say: Blessed are the poor! The world says: Happy are the rich, because you are worth as much as you own! Yet Christ says: That is a lie; blessed are the poor, because theirs is the kingdom of heaven, because they do not place their trust in what is merely transitory.

The issue of the poor was not an ideological one for Romero. They were not just a component of political history. For he saw them above all in their state of suffering. He himself lived at a hospital for poor, terminally-ill patients. At night he could hear their groans. In his homilies he asked the faithful to be more humane toward the sick:

> I live in a hospital and experience suffering very close at hand, the groans of pain during the night, the sadness of those who are admitted.... The Church will always have a very special mystical view of suffering, which no medical technique used by doctors and nurses and no hospital, however well-equipped, can ever give. These centers, these techniques, often objectify people; in other words, they make the sick person a thing. From now on he is no longer called by his name, just by a number, patient number so-and-so, as though he were some irrational creature. They forget that the patient is first of all a person, one who needs affection, charity, tenderness of heart. It is not enough for a nurse to be very skilled in giving injections and transfusions but then to treat the patient carelessly. Let this hour of [prayer and] compassion for the patients be a call to the doctors, the nurses, and the hospital to humanize with ever greater delicacy this mission of those who are dealing, not with an animal or a thing, but with a human being.

Romero proclaimed for himself and for his Church a preferential option for the poor. At the same time he was convinced that the poor had to convert as well:

> The Church does not say that everyone who is poor or oppressed is just, even though she never forgets that the grace of redemption is offered to them preferentially by the Redeemer himself. And because the Church knows that among those who lack material goods there is also much sin, she strives to help the people to overcome inveterate vices ... machismo, alcoholism, irresponsibility toward family, the exploitation of the poor by the poor, local rivalries, and many other sins.

For Romero, no category of Christians is exempt from the need to convert. The preferential option for the poor did not presume, he wrote, "an uncritical partiality in favor of the poor and a kind of contempt for the wealthy classes." The poor were favored by God but were not assured of salvation just because they were poor.

As in the years before he was appointed archbishop, *liberación, salvación, redención* were synonymous, interchangeable terms for Romero. In this way he incorporated *liberación*, an everyday word in Latin American Catholicism, into the more classical theological thought in which he had been trained, and into the thought of the popes. In August 1978, a reporter asked him whether his theological thought was based on liberation theology, and Romero replied: "Yes, it rests on liberation theology." Yet he added, "there are two types of that theology, one that relies only on earthly things and desires an immediate solution, and another that emanates from the message of Jesus, who comes to take away the sin of the world." He added that he "relied on the second type," stressing "that his theological thought was the same as that of Paul VI, described in the Apostolic Exhortation *Evangelii Nuntiandi*." In a pastoral letter Romero explains this statement as follows:

> When we fight for human rights, freedom, and dignity, when we are convinced that it is a ministry of the Church to care for those who are hungry, for those who have no school, for those who suffer marginalization, we are not turning aside from God's promise to free us from sin. . . . The Pope wrote this beautiful sentence, which we find in *Evangelii Nuntiandi*: "The Church strives always to insert the Christian struggle for liberation into the universal plan of salvation." What does this mean? The Church continues to work out God's plan of salvation. She has not turned aside from it. When she sees in the peoples of America the yearning for liberation, she incorporates this yearning, this struggle for Christian liberation, into Christ. She tells those who work for

liberation that a liberation without faith, without Christ, without hope—a violent, revolutionary liberation—is not effective, is not authentic. It has to start from redemption in Christ, redemption from sin. Laws and structures would be useless if human beings were not renewed interiorly, repenting of their own sins and striving to live a more just life.

Archbishop Romero regarded with definite sympathy the efforts of the Salvadoran people to achieve *liberación* from its historical evils: hunger, poverty, social injustice, violence. At the same time, he maintained that any authentic, integral liberation was chiefly concerned with sin, selfishness, wickedness. The "three forces" that brought about true liberation were not earthly, political, and military, but spiritual: "the spirit of poverty, the sense of God, our firm hope in the mystery of Christ." When popular political organizations were discussed at a diocesan meeting in November 1979, Romero stated:

> These men from the organizations appear very involved in the work of liberating the people. We fully understand this, but it grieves us to think that this struggle is only immanent, concerned only with earthly, political, economic realities and forms of slavery. We can understand all this and be in solidarity with these efforts at liberation, but from our perspective, which is much more complete. That is because it starts with liberation from sin and lifts human beings to the dignity of children of God, heirs of God's eternity. Therefore we are better able to understand earthly liberations and to guide them toward the great liberation of Christ.

The balance between the two poles of this "liberation," one worldly and the other supernatural, was always delicate, because one referred to the other. Romero spoke of this in November 1977, in Apopa, to a community experiencing the trials of persecution:

> There is no salvation apart from Christ our Redeemer. And this redemption by Christ is not only a redemption that we await after

death; it is a redemption that is already at work in this life. The word that upsets so many people, liberation, is a reality of Christ's redemption.... Liberation means redemption, which means freedom for humanity from so many forms of slavery. Illiteracy is slavery. Hunger is slavery when you have nothing with which to buy food. Lack of shelter, not having a place to live, is slavery. Slavery, poverty, it all goes together. And when the Church preaches that Christ came to redeem the human race and that, thanks to this redemption, there should be no forms of slavery on earth, the Church is not preaching subversion or politics, nor is she Communist. The Church is preaching true redemption in Christ, who does not want us to be slaves but wants all human beings to be redeemed, and the rich and the poor to love each other as brothers.

Liberation without any reference to transcendence, however, was not credible:

We will all die, but those who believe in Christ will not die forever. In heaven we will sing the victory of immortality, in comparison with which all the struggles for earthly liberation are little skirmishes. The great liberation is Christ's. Anyone who incorporates his people's struggle for liberation into his Christian faith has the assurance of integral, complete, immortal liberation. Anyone who wishes to turn away from this Christian liberation and limit his struggle to temporal affairs, better wages, lower prices, changing those in political office, changing structures that tomorrow will already be outdated . . . all that is temporal, transitory.

The only solution was liberation from sin. So he preached in December 1977:

All nature groans under the weight of sin. What beautiful coffee plantations, what fine sugar cane fields, what lovely cotton plantations, what estates, what lands God has given us! How beautiful nature is! But when we see it groaning under oppression, iniquity, injustice, tyranny, then the Church grieves and awaits a liberation that will not only be material well-being, but the power of a God who will liberate from the sinful hands of men.

CHAPTER SIX

Romero and Rome

Ecclesiastical Jealousies

 When Romero became archbishop of San Salvador, the Salvadoran bishops had been afflicted by strife and discord for several years. Romero, with his compelling demands, was not the one who caused their divisions. They already existed. Beginning in the sixties, the minutes of CEDES reveal ongoing disagreements that went beyond the normal debates in a conference of bishops. Although common decisions were reached on internal Church matters, it was hard to reach agreements on initiatives concerning civil and political matters.

Romero had solidarity from the other bishops of CEDES only in the first months of his episcopal ministry, when Fathers Grande and Navarro were killed. In the summer of 1977, CEDES underwent a division similar to the one that occurred in the years of Chávez's episcopate. The archbishop of San Salvador and his auxiliary, Rivera Damas, were in opposition to the bishops of the smaller dioceses of the country. As an archbishop, too, Romero enjoyed the friendship and support of Rivera, who as of 1978 was no longer an auxiliary in San Salvador but the bishop of Santiago de María. On the other hand, the three suffragan bishops of the archdiocese, Alvarez in San Miguel, Aparicio in San Vicente, and Barrera in Santa Ana were definitely hostile toward Romero.

Because Rivera would be receiving a new assignment, Romero asked the Holy See for a new auxiliary for San Salvador, specifically Marco René Revelo. It was an unfortunate request. Revelo soon proved to be Romero's enemy: in CEDES he joined the majority that regularly spoke out against the initiatives of Romero and Rivera. On his own initiative, Revelo sent negative reports about Romero to Rome, and he spoke of him disparagingly, even in government circles. Revelo was among those who suggested the apostolic visit to San Salvador conducted by Bishop Antonio Quarracino in 1979 with a view to Romero's possible removal. Revelo was convinced that one day he would become the archbishop of the capital, and Quarracino's visit gave him high hopes.

The case of Revelo shows a certain naiveté on Romero's part in understanding people. Revelo, energetic and self-willed, was far from Romero's pastoral style. Yet at first Romero defended him with hierarchical loyalty against the diocesan clergy who opposed Revelo for political reasons. Romero thought of the Church as communion, and judging collaborators on their political opinions was unacceptable to him. But Revelo's hostility toward him eventually disappointed him. He dismissed him as vicar general and limited his duties to a single parish.

Alvarez, Aparicio, and Barrera blatantly showed their hostility toward Romero, for example by publishing pastoral letters opposed to Romero's, in order to assert contrary views on the same subjects. Aparicio intervened publicly against Romero in Puebla and on other occasions. He also attempted to boycott the possible award of the Nobel Prize to Romero. In their dioceses, Alvarez, Aparicio, and Barrera obstructed the circulation of Romero's diocesan newspaper, *Orientación*, because it reflected the archbishop's thinking. The faithful were advised not to listen to Romero's homilies on the radio. Priests were told not to travel to the archdiocese; in other words, to avoid contact with Romero. The three bishops openly criticized Romero in government circles, even though those circles were partly responsible for the persecution of the Church. After denouncing the persecution in the first few months of 1977, the three bishops had decided to deny it, explaining the killings of priests and catechists as foreseeable consequences of their militantly leftist positions. Barrera related in 1994:

> The President of the Republic summoned certain bishops who, as he knew, disagreed with *Monseñor* Romero's preaching, to consult them on what he could do in this [Romero's] case that was worrying the whole nation. The first ones expressed their opinions, and last of all I stated mine: "The only sure thing you can do is, with all respect, to put *Monseñor* on an airplane and send him abroad, taking into account that initially the press will make its comments but, ultimately, the case will be forgotten."

In May 1979 Alvarez, Aparicio, Barrera, and Revelo, in the context of ongoing efforts to discredit the archbishop with the Vatican authorities, sent a letter to Rome in which they blamed Romero for the violence in the country. If the government failed to restore order and security, as it would have liked, this was due to the defamatory campaign orchestrated by Romero, which presented the government as "a human rights violator and persecutor of the Church." The letter said that Romero had designed the pastoral approach of the archdiocese to incite class struggle, political extremism, revolution, and the seizure of power by Communism. The politicization brought about by Romero among the clergy and the faithful allegedly had produced an "alarming crisis of faith in El Salvador among priests, nuns, and lay people." The letter went on to say that: "The people wonder how it is possible for a pastor of the Church to support ruthless criminals who openly declare themselves Marxist-Leninists." Romero also allegedly misinterpreted the concept of "people of God." He identified it with the "politicized public" who applauded him in the cathedral and not with the entire ecclesial communion of the faithful people and the hierarchy. The letter even attributed to Romero the opinion that papal infallibility was derived from an infallibility belonging to the "people of God." Romero—the letter concluded—had betrayed Catholic theology. Therefore Romero was a heretic who should be condemned and deposed.

What caused so much hostility? Alvarez, besides being the bishop of San Miguel, was also a military ordinary. He loved to appear in an officer's uniform and approved the conduct of the military regime. Barrera was very old and traditional in his thinking. He was annoyed by the "*nuovismo*" [novel approaches across the board] with which many priests and lay faithful in El Salvador wanted to implement Vatican II. The fickle Aparicio was forever seeking the spotlight. But the very bad relations between Romero and the other Salvadoran bishops, except for Rivera Damas, were not due to differences in character. Romero himself had a difficult character that was impulsive and sometimes authoritarian. Nevertheless, strong characters can also agree if they want to. Was it then a political or theological issue? Alvarez, Aparicio, Barrera, and Revelo tended to have good relations with the State and the oligarchy. They were not interested in a renewal of the Church in the spirit of Vatican II. They explained the violent acts against the Church as a tragic consequence of "Marxist infiltration" into the Church itself. But not even politics or theology can explain the disagreement between Romero and his brother bishops. In the case of Aparicio, at least, it is possible to list a long series of public statements opposing the powerful authorities in El Salvador and the regime's violence, until 1977. When Romero expressed support, albeit only conditionally, for the government that resulted from the coup on October 15, 1979, which was opposed by the popular organizations on the left, the nuncio approved. The bishops who opposed it did not do the same. This was more than a dispute over principles.

The main reason for the disagreement was in fact a distinct feeling of envy of Romero, given his fame, his popularity, and his attractiveness to the clergy of other dioceses. Romero bitterly noted several times the "personal aversion" of the above-mentioned bishops toward him. They showed this by their preconceived attitudes, aggressiveness, rudeness, and resentment, and by their refusal to stand in solidarity when Romero's priests were killed and his diocesan institutions attacked. Romero's correspondence and the minutes of CEDES from 1977 to 1980 show this personal aversion. It wasn't ideas but jealousies, rivalries, antagonisms, and quarrels over jurisdiction that created division among the bishops. One of the accusations unfailingly leveled against Romero during meetings of CEDES was that he "interfered in other dioceses, causing division among the priests and pastoral malaise in those diocese." Or else it was said that "the priests now take their inspiration more from the archdiocese [of San Salvador] than from their bishops." Romero was reproached with being "vain."

Among other things, Romero was significantly younger than Aparicio, Alvarez, and Barrera. He had surpassed them in rank with an episcopal career that was not so much precocious as it was meteoric once it got off the ground, ending with Romero's appointment as head of the country's metropolitan archdiocese. Previously, Chávez, with his authoritative governing style, had provoked annoyance and envy among the bishops of the suffragan dioceses. Now, Romero reaffirmed, even more explicitly, the same pre-eminence of the archdiocese. Romero had been secretary of CEDES, carrying out duties for Aparicio, Alvarez, and Barrera, but now he was the most prestigious member of the conference.

Many priests and communities of the dioceses of Santa Ana, San Vicente, and San Miguel used to cite Romero, with public declarations of esteem and affection, contrasting him with their own ordinaries. In the initial phase of Romero's tenure as archbishop, CEDES had shown unity. The reaction to the murder of Rutilo Grande had been unanimous. The persecution of the Church had brought bishops closer to each other, but soon the "Romero phenomenon" could not be contained. His prestige, fame, and authority grew and caused frustration in the other bishops. They were estranged from their own priests and faithful who were attracted by Romero's personality. Alvarez, Aparicio, and Barrera could not do anything but oppose him personally.

To tone down the jealousies, Romero tried to moderate the enthusiasm of the clergy and the faithful of other dioceses in his regard. He was anxious to avoid the thunderous applause that used to greet him personally, so as not to arouse envy: "The Cathedral of San Miguel was packed with people. . . . I noticed that the bishops were anxious to put me on the sidelines, but the people, for their part, gave me a warm reception as we left the church. I was expecting this, and therefore I left last, so as not to offend my brothers with this kind of popular rivalry. . . ." It was not always easy to keep the people from applauding him. Romero's homilies, broadcast by radio, were punctuated by applause that all El Salvador could hear.

In his correspondence with Cardinal Baggio, who as Prefect of the Congregation of Bishops, asked him to strive for the unity of the bishops' conference, Romero initially stressed the irrevocable nature of the "demands of the Gospel and of conscience," which could not be sacrificed on the altar of an artificial unity. Later, at the urging of the Pope, Baggio, and various nuncios, Romero took steps to remedy the disunity, without swerving from his pastoral approach, which he considered in keeping with God's will. In July 1979, before a meeting of CEDES, he wrote a reconciliatory circular letter to the other bishops. There had been weeks of great violence in the country, with two massacres of protesters, the assassinations of about twenty unionized teachers, the murders of more priests, police officers, and government ministers. Romero asked the bishops to take note of the tragic nature of the situation and to unite so as to prevent more bloodshed. "Has the disunity of us bishops perhaps facilitated the increased repression, the spiral of violence, and the fact that many crimes go unpunished?" Romero then turned to the Salvadoran bishops who disagreed with him, inviting them to consider their own shortcomings in order to find unity "leaving aside our own differences and limitations, which appear small when compared to the magnitude of the tragedy of our country."

Romero had scruples of conscience. During his last retreat he noted: "My sins . . . [against episcopal] collegiality: contempt, murmuring, pride, omissions, stubbornness." In fact Romero's responsibilities [in regard to collegial unity] were no greater than those of the other bishops. Initially he had not been willing to mediate, considering his course of action unquestionably right. He had acted in CEDES with his authority as archbishop, underestimating the frustration of the suffragan bishops who had greater seniority and did not want to appear inferior. Then bitterness and resignation entered into his relations with Alvarez, Aparicio, Barrera, and Revelo. He believed in conscience that he could not sacrifice his "consistently evangelical line" "just to honor an apparent unity." In his fourth pastoral letter he pointed out the "preferential option for the poor, understood in the Gospel sense" as the "key" to overcoming ecclesiastical divisions. He hoped that new appointments would gradually change the balance within CEDES. He wrote confidentially to Cardinal Lorscheider in January 1980:

> The disunity of the bishops' conference is very painful and sad, and a scandal for the faithful. [Except for *Monseñor* Rivera] the others do not implement thoroughly what the documents of the Church demand of us, and hence we are very far from having "participation and communion." Alert, well-formed Christians regard this situation with great anxiety. . . . The Holy See will know what must be done in this very delicate state of affairs. It is certain that we need new, different bishops. The documents of the Church and the situation in our country require appointees who are better suited to shape the image of the Latin American Church which has made a "preferential option for the poor."

The bishops opposed to Romero made no attempt at all to reach a *modus vivendi* with him. They had no competing programs or initiatives to debate. Because they greatly disliked Romero, they wanted him to be removed from office and they provoked him. They felt strong because they held the majority in CEDES. They argued that the archbishop was unorthodox, insane, severely ill psychologically, and that he had been brainwashed by his advisers, especially the Jesuits. The archbishop was a dangerous man who had to be stopped. The unity of the Church of El Salvador would return when Romero was gone.

"Courage, You Are in Charge!"

Romero made four visits to Rome as archbishop of San Salvador. They were genuine pilgrimages: each time Romero was profoundly moved to be in what he called "mother, teacher, homeland," and to pray at the tombs of the popes in the crypt of Saint Peter's. But they were also indispensable trips of ecclesiastical polity, in defense of his own actions. The first three Roman visits were variously marked by joys and worries. The last trip was the happiest and filled him with "deep serenity." In any case, Archbishop Romero insisted on the "wonderful experience of the Eternal City, ever ancient and ever new, promoter of universal faith." His visits to Rome aroused "apostolic courage" within him, even though in the Curia he met with varying degrees of understanding. This caused Romero suffering, but his idea of Rome remained very exalted: "They do not understand me, but Christ is behind them."

Rutilio Grande was assassinated right after Romero became archbishop. At that time the episode of the *misa única* saw Romero and the nuncio Gerada in open conflict. Although relations between the two had been good, they then became difficult. In Gerada's opinion, Romero "veered one hundred eighty degrees" after Rutilio Grande's death. It was the beginning of Romero's ecclesiastical problems with Rome as well, which Gerada represented locally. The nuncio was trying to maintain good relations with the government. So he publicly contradicted the line taken by Romero, who had decided to keep a safe distance from the civil authorities until serious investigations into the cases of murdered priests had been carried out and the military had stopped repressing the populace. Gerada reasoned as a diplomat, Romero as a shepherd. He believed, and he told Gerada clearly, that his office as local ordinary was superior to that of nuncio. Therefore Gerada ought to have followed

Romero and not vice versa. Gerada was surprised: he had worked for the appointment of Romero to San Salvador but soon began working to remove him. As early as March 1978, he suggested that Rome replace him with an apostolic administrator. In turn, Romero had no esteem for Gerada. He considered him a vague, colorless personality. Romero would have wanted the nuncio to stand by him stout-heartedly in asking the government leaders to obey the laws and to seek justice. In theory, the archbishop felt that he was in communion with Rome and that he was putting the magisterium into practice. But the nuncio, who represented Rome, was not on his side, and this embittered Romero. In the court of public opinion, the disagreement with Gerada made Romero appear to be at odds with Rome. His enemies emphasized this to discredit him.

In December 1978 Bishop Antonio Quarracino [of Avellaneda, Argentina], conducted the apostolic visitation in San Salvador. Gerada had asked for this when he had presented the situation to Baggio, Prefect of the Congregation of Bishops, which had to take the initiative, provided of course that the Pope agreed. Perhaps Baggio himself was already convinced that the serious step of a visitation was needed, bombarded as he was with anti-Romero messages from various ecclesiastical and political circles of El Salvador. Gerada took advantage of the apostolic visitation by Quarracino to propose that the Holy See replace Romero with his candidates, if it should decide to take any measures concerning the archdiocese.

In frequent meetings with the presidents, with Molina, and then with General Romero, the nuncio lamented the persecution of the Church, asked for less repressive policies, and called for moderation. But he did so without backbone, without a strong voice, betraying his disagreement with Romero. One can imagine what was heard by politicians who were accustomed to coarse barracks language. He also found that no one listened to him in CEDES when he tried to restore unity there. If Romero saw no authority in Gerada, the outcome shows that the other bishops attributed even less to him. Gerada continuously recommended prudence and asked that any criticism of the government be made softly (*"de maneras suaves"*). He ended up being haunted by a feeling of helplessness. After the meeting between Romero and John Paul II, in May 1979, Gerada was ordered to improve his relationship with Romero. He obeyed even though he continued to think that removing Romero would solve many Church-State problems.

The conflict with Gerada that developed after the death of Rutilio Grande worried Romero. In a memorandum for the Secretariat of State dated March 29, 1977, he retraced the latest events. Romero explained that the purpose of the *misa única* had been to prompt the diocese to reflect on what had happened, using the light of Scripture and the documents of the magisterium. In particular, the *misa única* was supposed to manifest visibly the unity of the Church and of the diocese. It was to emphasize the particular value of the Catholic priesthood, which had been profaned by the assassination of Father Grande and the expulsion of other priests. At the beginning of April 1977, just three weeks after the murder of the Jesuit, Romero went to Rome to inform the authorities personally about the events and to "manifest his intention to reinforce his communion and that of the whole archdiocese with the Holy See." The highlight of his first trip to Rome as archbishop was his meeting with Paul VI, following the Wednesday general audience. The Pope was affectionate with Romero, offered words of encouragement, blessed the photo of Rutilio Grande, and said to him: "Courage, you are the one in charge!" Romero left the meeting heartened.

In the following months, those in Rome started to talk frequently about El Salvador and Romero. In June, the Secretary of State, Cardinal Villot, wrote to Gerada "with some concern." They had noted that "some positions taken by the archbishop" might be causing "division among the faithful" and a "clash with the authorities," according to information coming from other Salvadoran bishops who were critical of Romero.

At the end of the year, Romero wrote to Villot to inform him of the preparations for the World Day of Peace on January 1, 1978. In these letters Romero stressed the impetus given to the "evangelizing and pastoral mission in the archdiocese." He added that although the Church of San Salvador was the target of violence and intimidation, it condemned those who would have liked to respond with force, for the Church was inspired by the Gospel and the papal magisterium. It therefore fulfilled the Pope's teaching: "No to violence, yes to peace." Citing *Evangelii Nuntiandi*, which Romero often referenced at the time, he emphasized the joy of evangelizing even through tears. He pointed out non-violent opposition to violence as a specifically Christian virtue. Villot replied with a polite yet demanding letter:

> For your part, Your Excellency, you will not cease to consider how urgent and necessary it is for you, under the present circumstances and taking advantage of the work of the Papal Representative, to contribute and work always toward finding a common understanding with your brothers in the episcopate, truly re-establishing an ongoing understanding with them in view of a fruitful dialogue with the governmental authorities, just as you yourself desire. Indeed, all of this could, on the one hand, help obtain a more serene, balanced, and impartial vision of the country's conditions and, on the other hand, could efficaciously favor the search for an equitable and peaceful solution to the numerous problems that afflict the nation.

Two aspects of the Salvadoran situation worried the authorities at the Holy See: the relationship between the Church and the government, and the disunity of the episcopate.

Clarifications at the Vatican

Romero knew that he was the object of attacks in the Vatican. With his closest collaborators he studied ways to neutralize the negative information, in particular, by making sure that testimonies of people favorable to him arrived at the Curia. Moreover, Rome was already receiving letters, complaints, appeals, and documents that the clergy of San Salvador independently produced against the nuncio and the bishops opposed to Romero, although these efforts were counterproductive. This documentation described the ecclesiastical conflicts during the political crisis of El Salvador in vehement and emphatic terms. It was common in those years to publicly voice the reasons for one's own ideological cause as though they were sacred truths that would persuade anyone. Those who compiled these combative materials hurried to send them to Rome for the record, convinced that they would resolve the problems. It was a naive approach, because the aggressive language of these materials alone caused discomfort in Roman circles.

In what Romero used to call "the Secretariats of the Pope," Cardinal Baggio, Prefect of the Congregation for Bishops, had the best grasp of the Salvadoran situation. Baggio also presided over the Pontifical Commission for Latin America (of which Romero was a member) and had begun his career in El Salvador, of all places. He had arrived there in 1939, at the age of twenty-seven, as an advisor of the nunciature. Opinions and comments about Romero also reached Baggio from Salvadoran circles with which he was personally acquainted. On May 16, 1978, Baggio wrote to Romero inviting him to come to Rome for a "definitive clarification."

Romero's second trip to Rome as archbishop took place from June 17–30, 1978. As Romero had guessed, this trip was marked by the need to refute the negative reports that had been circulated against him. The first meetings in the Curial dicasteries led him to leave a note with Paul VI during the audience that the Pope had granted him. Romero wrote, among other things: "I lament, Holy Father, the fact that in the comments shown me here in Rome regarding my pastoral conduct, a negative interpretation prevails. This coincides exactly with the powerful forces in my archdiocese that are seeking to curb and discredit my apostolic efforts."

A visit to the tombs of the Apostles Peter and Paul was Romero's "primary concern" as soon as he began his stay in Rome: "I entrusted to the protection of Saint Peter and Saint Paul my faith and the fidelity of the archdiocese to the teachings and guidelines of the Holy Church of Christ." After that came his most important meeting, the one with Baggio. It was an hour-long conversation. Baggio did not conceal from Romero the fact that the Salvadoran bishops, except for Rivera Damas, had asked for his removal. The conversation began almost brutally, as Romero recalled to the same cardinal in a long memorandum:

> Your Eminence began by expressing a feeling of frustration, shared by several highly respected persons who had supported my appointment by preferring me to *Monseñor* Rivera. Among these I recall that you mentioned Cardinal Casariego and Father Carlos Siri. I think that Your Eminence also mentioned your personal preference for *Monseñor* Rivero, in agreement with *Monseñor* Chávez. You also recalled the dissatisfaction of my brother bishops in El Salvador who have even asked for my removal and the disappointment of many priests who hoped to collaborate with me and who now "feel marginalized." I am allegedly "brainwashed," obeying a group of "fawning" priests who have deified me ("Urioste, Fabián Amaya, Jesús Delgado . . . and others not worth mentioning"). What was expected of me was an attitude of equanimity, serenity and prudence, not the aggressiveness with which I am acting.

Romero felt the need to say that he too recognized that Rivera had a kind of "superiority." He asserted that he had never refused to dialogue with his priests and diocesan employees. He insisted that he did not feel "brainwashed" by adulators. Rather, he had "a clear awareness that [he] had made [his] own decisions in governing the diocese," while also taking care to ask priests and laity for advice according to their competencies. "The Lord's Mystical Body grows in an obedience that is shared responsibility." He denied that he had had a "conversion" and that he had ever spoken about himself in those terms—something that he had been accused of by the Salvadoran bishops who were his adversaries. He said that the accusations of Marxism that had been leveled against many priests by bishops like Aparicio or Alvarez were a form of "an obsession." If some priests blundered in the political arena or favored ambiguous expressions that seemed to recommend "violence or partisan politics," it was better to try to correct them with "an approach of fraternal trust" than to treat them as reprobates and to censure them publicly.

Baggio had also heard rumors critical of the two murdered priests, Grande and Navarro. They had been presented to him as violent men devoted to politics. In this regard Romero, indignant at the insult to the memory of their "final testimony of immolation," lamented that Baggio should pay attention to disgraceful rumors. He said that the two assassinated priests had "limitations" and "shortcomings" resulting from their restricted environment, yet had "sincere love for the truth of the Church." Furthermore he denied that he had praised them fanatically, as some had insinuated.

Baggio was anxious to clarify the relationship between Romero and his auxiliary Revelo, who had sent to Rome a list of complaints about his ordinary. Revelo thought that Romero was guilty of having sidelined him. Actually Romero had done the opposite, pressuring the clergy, who disliked Revelo, to acknowledge his authority. Baggio confirmed a statement made by Revelo, who had told Romero that he had been assigned to San Salvador as an auxiliary in order to curb the archbishop. Romero felt betrayed, and he reacted. How could he continue to work for "a cordial relationship" with Revelo, "when both of them knew that it was, instead, a relationship of vigilance and restraint"? Romero also had to defend his own preaching, the subject of complaints from his opponents. Baggio had received from San Salvador the texts of Romero's homilies that his detractors considered theologically reprehensible. To Romero's relief, the cardinal said that he had found no "doctrinal errors" in them. The meeting with the Prefect of the Congregation for Bishops touched on the relations between Church and State, the seminary, the conduct of religious men and women. Baggio criticized an honorary degree that the Jesuits at Georgetown University had granted to Romero, saying it was an obvious "political trap." ("It does you no honor.") Lastly, the question of his removal was addressed:

> Finally, Your Eminence mentioned to me the petition for my removal submitted by my brother bishops and the possibility thereof. And with the same simplicity as in our meeting, I put it in writing: if it is for the good of the Church, with great pleasure I will hand over to someone else this difficult government of the Archdiocese. However, as long as it is my responsibility, I will try only to be pleasing to the Lord and to serve his Church and his people according to my conscience in the light of the Gospel and of the magisterium.

On June 21 Romero met with the Pope. In his own description of the meeting he notes that Paul VI was not stiff, but rather:

> . . . cordial, broad, generous, the emotion of the moment was not meant to be remembered word for word; but the main ideas of his words could be summed up as: "I understand your difficult task. It is a work that can be misunderstood and requires much patience

and much strength. I know that not everyone thinks the same as you do and, under the circumstances that your country is living, it's difficult to have unanimity of thought. Nevertheless, go forward with courage, patience, strength, and hope." He promised he would pray very much for me and my diocese. And he told me to make every effort toward unity and that if there was anything he could personally do, he would be happy to do so. He referred later to the people saying that he was familiar with them since he had worked in the Secretariat of State about fifty years ago and he knew the people to be generous as well as hardworking, and that today [the people were] suffering greatly and wanted to claim their rights. He told me we had to help the people, work for them, but never with hatred or fostering violence, but rather to act always from a foundation of love. [He told me] to help the people feel the value of their suffering, to preach peace, and to help the people know how much the Pope loves, prays for, and works for them. He also spoke about difficulties that can only be overcome with love.

In the following days Romero returned to justify his conduct, especially with Casaroli at the Secretariat of State. Casaroli had on his desk documentation that Romero had delivered to the Pope, with annotations that Romero thought were in the handwriting of Paul VI. Eager to improve the relations between Romero and the government, Casaroli arranged a meeting between the archbishop of San Salvador and the Salvadoran ambassador to the Holy See, Prudencio Llach. Casaroli thus set the table for dialogue between Church and State. Romero courteously obliged. When the time came for him to return to El Salvador, Romero was serene. He had realized the extent of the criticism against him, but he had been encouraged by his audience with Paul VI and by his various meetings in Rome. He had spoken about his work to Cardinal Pironio and the Jesuit Superior General, Pedro Arrupe, who also supported him. Romero spent his last two days in Rome participating, as a simple pilgrim, in the feast of Saints Peter and Paul:

> I went to Saint Peter's when they were singing vespers for the patrons Saint Peter and Saint Paul. The two of them are patron saints of Rome. Here also the solemn chant of vespers, in a festive atmosphere, in a universal concurrence, that fills the choir of the basilica, has brought back so many memories. And there, next to the tomb of Saint Peter, I prayed the Apostles' Creed asking God for the fidelity and the clarity to believe and preach the same faith of the apostle Saint Peter. . . . Despite returning to my country, I am homesick for Rome. Rome is home for the one who has faith and has a sense of the Church. Rome is the country of all Christians. The Pope, who is the true father of all, is there. I felt so close to him.

Romero had not realized that his second trip to Rome as archbishop occurred while the slanderous attacks against him were reaching their climax. Hence his ecclesiastical position was shaky and remained so until his next trip to Rome in May 1979. His friendship with Paul VI had protected Romero. Baggio had serious doubts about his work because of the flood of negative reports that arrived in Rome, starting with those from the nuncio, Gerada. But Romero's relationship with the Pope served as an umbrella for him. However Paul VI died on August 6, 1978. That was the year of the three Popes. Pope Paul VI's successor, John Paul I, passed away a month after his election, and then Karol Wojtyła was elected. Seven difficult months went by before Romero established a relationship with John Paul II.

The Apostolic Visitation

In August 1978, two different pastoral letters about the popular political organizations—one by Romero and Rivera and the other by the bishops opposed to them—clearly showed the division within the Salvadoran episcopate. Romero did not provoke the incident. He had forwarded to the other bishops, for their information, the draft of his pastoral letter well in advance of its publication, inviting them to sign it jointly. The reply was an alternative pastoral letter on the same subject, which the other bishops published to repudiate him. This scandalous division increased the resolve in Roman circles to take action.

Pope John Paul II was elected on October 16, 1978. On November 7, 1978, Romero sent to the new Pope a letter that was unfortunate, to say the least. After briefly retracing the events of his episcopal governance and the conditions in the country, the letter continued in an entirely negative tone. Romero denounced "the very persistent and not very intelligent pressures" of the nuncio to make him appear to be "in union with a government that has lost all its credibility with the people and whose apparent friendship with the archbishop would make the latter, too, lose the confidence which, thank God, he enjoys among the people." He therefore requested that Gerada limit himself to diplomatic activities, avoiding pastoral interference. Then Romero severely criticized Bishops Alvarez, Barrera ("he is already a seventy-six-year-old man and he never opted for a pastoral approach of serious, evangelical commitment to his people"), Aparicio ("fickle, vain and self-seeking . . . accomplice of the persecutorial methods [of the government]"), and Revelo. In discussing the latter, Romero criticized Cardinal Baggio, who had defended the auxiliary bishop when he had refused to be integrated into the diocesan pastoral ministry. Moreover Romero complained that Revelo was watching over him on behalf of the Congregation for Bishops. Regarding the upcoming Puebla Conference, Romero expressed fear that it was ill-prepared ("fears and even convictions that it was about to 'extinguish the Spirit' with human schemes"). Then he returned to the theme of the Salvadoran episcopate. Romero stressed how important it was to avoid promoting to the episcopate some "very negative" priests nominated by Aparicio and Barrera. He also begged for the removal of Revelo from San Salvador, because of "the impossibility of achieving a friendly collaboration." He added that Revelo was not "fit to govern a diocese."

The letter could only have adverse effects for Romero. The newly-elected Pope, without any experience of Salvadoran matters, could not evaluate it on its merits. Even if he tried to do so, he could not help but get a painful impression of someone unknown to him. And this first act of a personal relationship yet to be established was to express vitriolic criticism of many priests, bishops, and cardinals, including some of his closest collaborators, such as Baggio. Anxious and impulsive, Romero designed the letter like a courtroom cross-examination, so that the higher authority, the Pope, might acquit him of the charges leveled against him. Twice already Paul VI had encouraged him and, in a certain sense, extricated him from the plots of his adversaries. But Paul VI knew Romero rather well. John Paul II, on the contrary, had never met Romero and may not have had more than a merely geographical view of El Salvador.

The letter to the Pope was swiftly examined by two prelates who were closely following the events of the Salvadoran Church, Baggio and Casaroli. At the conclusion of that letter Romero asked "that investigations about candidates for the episcopate and about my pastoral conduct be carried out not only through the nunciature, but also through other channels that are better acquainted with our ecclesial and national situation." The further investigations confidently but unwisely suggested by Romero would be translated, in a few days, into the decision to send an apostolic visitor to San Salvador. This decision, advocated by Gerada for a long time and endorsed by Baggio, was probably accelerated by a brief but alarming meeting that Revelo managed to have with John Paul II during those same days. The Pope, however, emerged from it convinced that he had to know Romero personally before making irreversible decisions about him.

In that same month of November, Romero dismissed his auxiliary Revelo from the post of vicar general. He listed the reasons for his decision in a letter to Baggio, with specific references to canon law. Romero's "greater disappointment" with Revelo had been caused by the latter's "non-existent cooperation in the governance and pastoral ministry of the archdiocese." "I have never felt any support from him, any service . . . never any fraternal communication." Romero's disillusionment had reached its peak with the change of statutes of the national organization CARITAS. The purpose was to transfer it from the jurisdiction of the archdiocese of San Salvador to that of CEDES. Revelo had signed the abrogation of the rights of the archdiocese with the agreement of the governing authorities, taking advantage of Romero being sick. The government had then refused to invalidate the documentation, which Romero said was illegitimate. Revelo's conduct in this affair was for Romero "a clear sign meant to gratify persons who are openly opposed to me and, what is worse, a dangerous precedent of interference by the civil authority in the authority or autonomy of the Church."

On December 14, 1978, the Argentine bishop Antonio Quarracino suddenly showed up in San Salvador, without Romero being informed in advance. He was sent as an apostolic visitor by the Congregation for Bishops, which is to say by Baggio. Quarracino conducted the most classic and scrupulous of all ecclesiastical inspections. He visited the various institutions of the archdiocese, and he listened to people who favored Romero and to those who opposed him. In particular, he gathered information on the relations between Romero and Revelo. He was polite and kept his impressions to himself. Romero thought that it was a good visit, in the sense that it would confirm his pastoral approach.

The outcome of Quarracino's visit was not what Romero had imagined. The Argentine bishop was impressed by the harsh contrast between the two factions that he found in the Salvadoran Church. While not blaming Romero, he proposed appointing an apostolic administrator *sede plena*[1] to San Salvador. At the same time he suggested replacing the nuncio, Gerada, whom he thought unequal to the task. Quarracino also suggested retiring the bishops opposed to Romero or reducing their powers, replacing them with a new generation of young prelates who were strangers to the divisions within the Salvadoran Church.

Those in the Vatican hesitated to implement Quarracino's recommendations. The case of the Salvadoran archdiocese needed deeper scrutiny. The only one who informed Romero about the proposal to appoint an apostolic administrator in his place was John Paul II, during an audience on May 7.

Unaware of the results of Quarracino's visit, Romero was in Mexico from January 22 to February 16, 1979, for the Conference of Latin American Bishops in Puebla. The bishops broke into twenty-one study commissions to prepare the final documents of the conference. Of these, Romero chose the one on "evangelization and human promotion," which was supposed to also deal with liberation theology. According to the testimony of Câmara, who participated in the same commission, it set up its works with some flexibility. Romero participated in it without preconceived opinions, humbly giving up his views several times when the majority

---

1. An apostolic administrator *sede plena* takes authority over a diocese while the bishop remains in office. This is done only rarely when, for some reason, the bishop cannot govern the diocese on his own. —*Ed.*

disagreed. Moreover he actively helped draft the summary of the commission's work.

Romero's secretary in Puebla recalls that during the business meetings of the Conference the archbishop was, in keeping with his character, intimidated, "almost inhibited," seized by "silent modesty." He made no move to meet Baggio, much less John Paul II. Romero did not lobby for himself in an environment that he felt was much larger and holier than his own person. To his surprise, he found instead that he was a media star. The journalists applauded him during the press conference. They chanted loudly: "Nobel! Nobel!" Romero represented a persecuted Church and he was a human rights advocate. Two days before he left for Mexico, the National Guard of San Salvador attacked a rectory in the village of El Despertar at night, where a retreat was taking place, brutally killing a priest and four youngsters. The incident led to escalating violence: a guerrilla group dynamited a military complex, causing about twenty deaths, in retaliation for the massacre in El Despertar. For this reason, too, Romero was surrounded in Puebla by newspaper and television reporters.

Romero and John Paul II

In late April 1979, Romero went to Rome for a beatification ceremony.[2] He took this opportunity to meet John Paul II and, as he noted, "to complete the report of the apostolic visitor." One way he did this was by delivering copious documentation directly to the

---

2. Romero went to Rome for the beatification of Francisco Coll Guitart, a Spanish Dominican priest who founded the Dominican Sisters of the Annunciation of the Blessed Virgin. He was later canonized by Pope Benedict XVI. —*Ed.*

Pope. Romero saw this trip as a continuation of his exchange of information with Rome, which had started with his letter to the new Pope on November 7, 1978, and with Quarracino's visit the following December. He supposed that Rome had received new negative reports about him. Indeed, the fact that he had not been removed after the apostolic visit had rekindled efforts to discredit him with the Roman authorities. On the eve of his trip to Rome, his third as archbishop, Romero proclaimed in the cathedral: "I will follow all that the Pope says. I already know that out there lay many reports against me. There are a lot of reports that speak suspiciously of my pastoral work and I know that the Pope will ask me about that." A few weeks before his departure, Romero had requested an audience with the Pope. But he went through the wrong channel, that of Ambassador Llach, who was not well-disposed toward him. When John Paul II met him at a general audience on May 2, the Pope took the initiative in telling him that he wanted to speak to him in private, as though he didn't know that Romero wanted to have an audience.

Karol Wojtyła had been pope for more than six months and had already familiarized himself with the problems of Latin America, especially through his experience of the continental conference in Puebla. He had no direct knowledge of the situation in El Salvador, but he was eager to talk to the man who had been described to him in controversial terms. The Pope knew that Romero had had an understanding with Paul VI. At his meeting with the Pope, Romero appeared carrying a large bundle of documents about El Salvador and his own work, which he handed over after a brief explanation. Wojtyła observed that pastoral work in the political environment of El Salvador was "extremely difficult" and urged "a very balanced and prudent approach, especially when making concrete accusations," in order to avoid mistakes. Romero replied that "there are situations, such as the case of Father Octavio, in which one has to be very specific because the injustice and violence had been very specific." This met with the Pope's approval. According to Romero's own account, John Paul II then went on to speak about the

> ... situation in Poland, where he had to face a non-Catholic government and with which it was necessary to build up the Church despite the difficulties. He gave great importance to the unity of the episcopate. Recalling again his pastoral ministry in Poland, he said that this was the main problem: maintaining the unity of the episcopate. I made sure he understood that this was what I desired most, but that I knew that unity must not be feigned. Rather it should be based on the Gospel and on the truth. He referred to the report of the apostolic visitation of Bishop Quarracino, who recognized the very delicate situation and recommended—as a response to the deficiencies in pastoral work and the lack of unity among the bishops—the appointment of an apostolic administrator with full authority (*sede plena*). Upon concluding our visit, in which he gave me the opportunity to share my thoughts and he shared his opinions, he invited me to take a photo together.

Romero was anxious to convince the Pope of the gravity of the situation in El Salvador and of the merits of his pastoral decisions. During the first encounter with a Pope with whom he was unacquainted, it might have been appropriate to seek to establish first of all some personal rapport, if only on the basis of the history that Romero represented. Perhaps Romero was expecting that John Paul II, as the supreme authority of the Church, was going to make his irrevocable judgment on the situation in El Salvador.

The Pope understood the Salvadoran archbishop's anxious state of mind. He gave no definitive answers to the questions Romero posed. He made comparisons with Poland which Romero, at the time, did not understand. The Pope likened the Salvadoran government to the Polish Communist government. This comparison with the Communist regimes of Eastern Europe was unflattering for the Salvadoran government. The Pope gave Romero some advice derived from his personal experience in the Eastern Bloc. In crisis situations with civil authorities, the Pope said, it was necessary first of all to strengthen the Church, in order to resist and then to take the initiative from steadfast, strong positions.

John Paul II did not call into question Romero's judgment regarding the situation in El Salvador and his denunciation of the regime's hostility toward the Church. Rather than directly oppose the political authority, it was wiser to strengthen the Church. During those same months, John Paul II was asking the same of the Catholic churches in Eastern Europe. He considered their cohesion and internal strength indispensable if they were to confront the regimes. In light of this, the Pope adopted as his own the recommendation that Paul VI had already made to Romero, that he should strive first and foremost for the unity of the episcopate. During the confrontation between Church and State in Poland, that unity was decisive, and it could be in El Salvador also. Andrea Riccardi, a biographer of John Paul II, wrote: "The unity of the episcopate is the priority, a must, for Wojtyła. Throughout his pontificate, the Pope untiringly recommended unity among the bishops, especially when confronting strong political authorities." In insisting only on the unity of the episcopate and in accepting Romero's negative judgment on the government, the Pope expressed a sensibility different from that of other Vatican circles, which were asking Romero to restore good relations with the government.

During the meeting, John Paul II informed Romero that the report Quarracino had written suggested appointing an apostolic administrator *sede plena* in San Salvador. Romero left the meeting a little uncertain, admitting that he was "pleased" but at the same time "concerned." It seemed to him that he had underestimated the negative reports on his account. He pondered what the Pope had recommended to him: "courage and boldness" but "tempered with prudence and the necessary balance." He gave the impression that he "did not feel completely satisfied with the meeting." Nevertheless he told himself that it had been "extremely helpful" because the Pope had been "very honest": "I have learned that one cannot always expect total approval." The next day a mood of "depression" took over. The Pope's consent was very important to Romero. John Paul II had been undecided at times—mostly due to a need to understand the problems that brought him there—and furthermore he had informed him about Quarracino's negative conclusions. It was enough to shake Romero and throw him into depression. Rome and the magisterium of the Church, embodied in the figure of the Pope, was the guiding star for his faith. The meaning of the Pope's recommendations probably escaped Romero. In those moments he correctly supposed that his problems with Rome had originated from the nuncio Gerada, who had given inaccurate reports.

Judging from later developments, the outcome of the meeting with John Paul II was not as negative as Romero tended to believe. If nothing else, his meeting with Baggio, the day after the one with the Pope, might have suggested to Romero that John Paul II was helping him within the Curia. Romero was amazed by Baggio's cordiality. He was expecting from him "some severity" as in their previous meeting in June 1978. They discussed the apostolic visit and the possible appointment of an apostolic administrator who, Baggio said, would not necessarily deprive Romero of his authority but rather support him. The cardinal had in mind a twofold ecclesiastical authority in the Church of San Salvador. One, in the person of Romero, would be directly responsible for the religious message. The other, the apostolic administrator, would be in charge of relations with the government and the other Salvadoran bishops. Yet the cardinal himself thought that such an appointment was "not a very practical solution" because they knew of no one capable of such a role, which presupposed a good understanding with Romero. Any decision in that regard was then "deferred." Romero assured him of "his best efforts to remedy the situation." Baggio cordially observed: "We are not dealing with one another as enemies, but as those who are working for the same cause and right now we are ninety percent in agreement. To reach one hundred percent is the truth; it is the Gospel." Romero expressed to Baggio his hope for a positive solution for himself and for the archdiocese, based on their common love for the Church.

Naturally, Romero continued to be tormented. He did not understand that the meeting with John Paul II and the judgment that the Pope had presumably passed on it had had the immediate effect of making the Curia less dependent on the criticism against Romero that arrived from overseas. The nuncio Gerada traveled to Rome the month after Romero's journey. As soon as he returned to San Salvador he wanted to meet Romero. "The nuncio," Romero noted, "told me that the Holy Father and the Sacred Congregation for Bishops are worried about the division among the Salvadoran episcopate and that they have great expectations in my collaboration to achieve unity." Gerada did not mention the relations between Church and State, a previous theme of conflict with Romero. Instead, he asked the archbishop "as a friend" to help him in the case of a priest in a difficult situation. Romero noted: "The nuncio proved to be very friendly and desired very much to collaborate in my challenging pastoral duties. I could tell that something had been said to him in Rome, for he was extremely friendly to me."

Romero had initially missed the relevance of the comparison between Poland and El Salvador made during the meeting with

Pope John Paul II. But he meditated on it, and a month later he again took up the subject while commenting on the first, triumphal visit of Karol Wojtyła to his homeland:

> Even in the worst catastrophes and under the worst regimes, the faith of the [Polish] people preserves their hope.... I am very glad to see the concurrence of the Pope's thoughts in Poland with those of the archdiocesan approach in San Salvador. The Pope says: "Normal relations between Church and State in Poland are connected with the cause of fundamental human rights." And he declares: "No authentic dialogue can take place"— the Supreme Pontiff said this—"unless the authorities respect the convictions of believers, guarantee all the rights of citizenship and also establish normal conditions for the Church's activity." What else have we been saying [in El Salvador]?

In the following months Gerada continued to be polite to Romero. He still had reservations about the archbishop, however, and would have liked to see Romero removed by Rome. Meanwhile, concerns about Romero's safety were increasing. The nuncio forwarded to him worrisome reports in this regard, which he had gathered from the presidency of the Republic. Romero said that they were credible, since he took seriously similar warnings that reached him from Rome shortly afterward. The Holy See offered Romero hospitality until the danger of being assassinated had passed, but Romero declined the offer.

"A Pastor's Greatest Glory"

In late January 1980, Romero took advantage of an opportunity to be in Europe—an honorary degree from the University of Louvain in Belgium—and returned to Rome. In planning his fourth trip to Rome as archbishop he had not requested a private audience with the Pope, for he was supposed to stay only two days. He wanted to pray in Saint Peter's and, if possible, to attend the general audience to greet the Pope, if only briefly. Romero had come to Europe chiefly for the academic ceremony in Louvain, but he had always devotedly visited the capital of Catholicism whenever he traveled to Europe. He didn't want to make an exception for the first time in his life. Once in Rome he felt ". . . the same emotion as always, for me Rome means returning to the crib, to our home, to the font, to the heart, to the head of our Church. I have asked the Lord to [help me] hold on to this faith and to adherence to the Rome Christ chose as the seat of his universal shepherd, the pope."

At the general audience on January 30, 1980, the Pope again took the initiative, as he had done the previous May. When the time came for final greetings to the attending bishops, Romero introduced himself and John Paul II told him: "Yes, I know you. I would like to talk to you after the audience: wait for me, please." The Pope received him "very warmly" in a small room adjoining the great Nervi Hall (now called the Paul VI Audience Hall). This is the account of the meeting recorded by Romero on the same day:

> The Holy Father told me: "I know the serious situation your country is going through, and I know that your apostolate is very difficult. You can count on my prayers: every day I pray for El Salvador. It is necessary to defend social justice and love for the poor a lot, tenaciously, but it is also necessary to be very careful about the ideologies that can seep into this defense of human rights, which in the long term are just as harmful to human rights." I replied: "Holy Father, I am glad to be in agreement, because I am seeking this balance: to defend social justice courageously, which is the weakest point in my country. To be with the people fully, but also to point out that there can be dangers in claims made without Christian sentiments." He told me that this was the balance that had to be maintained and that we should

always have trust in God. This is a summary of his thought; then he gave me a strong embrace, told me that he was with me, and gave me a special blessing for my people.

Before departing for Louvain, Romero had a meeting with the new secretary of state at the latter's request. Villot had recently died and Cardinal Casaroli had succeeded him. Casaroli warned Romero that the United States diplomats suspected him "of being part of a popular revolutionary line," but he added, "nevertheless, the Church must proceed, not so as to please earthly powers but [to act] according to her faith and her conscience in the Gospel." Casaroli expressed concern about possible ideological burdens that might result for the Salvadoran Church from any support for the "people's desire for justice." Romero told him that he shared this fear. So whenever he preached on social justice, he remained constantly on guard against the "danger of falling into foreign ideologies." Casaroli confirmed that he shared Romero's vision for El Salvador in that time of crisis. According to Romero, it was necessary to reject the political option of the right and to create an alliance among the healthy forces of the nation. *"¡Ese es el camino!"*[3] Casaroli had exclaimed at that point. Finally, Romero reiterated his intention to monitor the danger that the people's "Christian ideals" might be sacrificed to "a temporal liberation." Romero's relationship with the Vatican authorities seemed to be redefined. It was now as friendly as could be. In May 1979, Romero had left Rome without having understood that John Paul II had given him his confidence. In contrast, Romero returned from his last trip to Rome in a state of euphoria, strengthened by the full solidarity of the Pope, which had been expressed in personal,

---

3. "That is the way!" —*Ed.*

fraternal terms. Being so much better acquainted with the Pontiff, Romero could rely in the future on personal communication with him, and knew that he was in his thoughts and prayers. In the following weeks, Romero made several enthusiastic references in his Sunday homilies to his meeting with John Paul II. On March 2, he said: "Brethren, the greatest glory of a pastor is to live in communion with the Pope. For me the secret of the truth and effectiveness of my preaching is to be in communion with the Pope."

In March 1980, the nuncio in Costa Rica, Lajos Kada, was commissioned by the Holy See to speak to the Salvadoran bishops to lead them to greater unity. Gerada, about to conclude his tenure in Central America, felt powerless now. Kada, an energetic Hungarian, thought that Romero was chiefly to blame for the disunity in CEDES and made this clear to him. In any case, during the CEDES meeting on March 12, Kada realized that, unlike the other bishops, Romero showed determination to bring about unity.

A few days later, Romero was killed. His assassination took place when it became clear in San Salvador that the Holy See would not remove the archbishop from office. The circles hostile to Romero had been disappointed over the lack of a disciplinary intervention by the Holy See, and by the support the Pope had given him at their meeting on January 30, 1980.

Wojtyła never forgot Romero. When he traveled to El Salvador on March 6, 1983, during the civil war, he wanted to pray at his tomb in the cathedral. The Pope dramatically departed from an itinerary that was supposed to avoid commemorating the archbishop. The Pope's vehicle turned aside from the predetermined route and drove through deserted streets to arrive at the cathedral. It was closed, so they had to wait a few minutes at the door until someone found the keys. John Paul II could finally kneel at the tomb of the murdered archbishop. He exclaimed many times: "Romero is ours," reasserting the ecclesial, priestly, and religious character of Romero's life and death. "Almost on the evening after the assassination," as Rivera Damas would remark, the figure of Romero had undergone in public opinion a distorted interpretation that removed him from the religious sphere to turn him into a political symbol.

CHAPTER SEVEN

Romero's Final Days

Romero and the Revolutionary Government

On October 15, 1979, an almost bloodless coup brought down the government of General Carlos Humberto Romero. The Revolutionary Government was formed.[1]

It was made up of representatives from the army and from civil society. The two protagonists in the overthrow of the government, Colonels Adolfo Majano and Jaime Gutiérrez, did not have the same political vision. Majano cherished quasi-revolutionary

---

1. This government was called *Junta Revolucionaria de Gobierno*, abbreviated JRG or "Junta." —*Trans.*

designs and was the leader of a minority of young officers. Gutiérrez represented the institutional military. They felt that a new domestic political scene was needed, for fear that the recently victorious Sandinista revolution in Nicaragua might be contagious. The Junta's plan was based on the proclamation issued on October 15 by the military leaders of the coup. It envisaged freedom to organize political parties and labor unions, conditions for holding democratic elections, a fight against violence regardless of the source (it foresaw, among other things, the disbanding of ORDEN, the Democratic Nationalist Organization), the defense of human rights, broad agrarian reforms, and the nationalization of the banking and fiscal sectors and of foreign trade.

Although he was not a member of the Junta, Duarte, a sort of Salvadoran Perón, had returned from exile. He was reorganizing the Christian Democratic Party, which participated in the government. The Communist Party also supported the Junta. The progressive intellectuals of Central American University (UCA) rose to the occasion: moreover its young rector Mayorga was president of the Junta. On the other hand, it was opposed by the guerrilla groups and the popular organizations, in other words, by the leftist, revolutionary movement that had made inroads in the country due to the paralyzed democratic system.

Internally, the Junta was subjected to increasing pressure from the right-wing component of the army, which had gradually recovered from "Nicaragua Syndrome." This permitted limited reforms in exchange for permission to repress the allegedly ongoing Communist insurrection. The death toll climbed. In the weeks immediately after the coup, hundreds of demonstrators were killed or wounded by the military and the police during demonstrations in the public square. Now, instead of assassinations of individual political opponents, teachers, and union leaders, there were serial murders by "death squads." In the aftermath of October 15, Major Roberto D'Aubuisson, third-in-command in military intelligence, was dismissed from the service along with eighty other officers. But as he left office, he took with him the card file of adversaries and "Communists." On this basis the "death squads" continued the earlier repressive campaign in a clandestine way. He coordinated his activity with right-wing elements in the military.

The Junta did not succeed in controlling the actions of the army and the security forces. They were heightening tensions in the country, trying to restore the political balance to the perennial situation of a military government that ruled in concert with the oligarchy. But the right-wing military was not the only faction to pursue a strategy of conflict. The revolutionary left was against the Junta and its policy of reform. "All or nothing" was the sentiment of the militants among the guerrillas and in the popular organizations. They did not believe in the reforms because they came from above, not from the people, and because they were a surrogate for the revolution. After a short truce due to their surprise at the progressive character of the Junta, guerrilla groups and popular organizations strove to topple it, convinced that they were now in a political phase of insurrection. They organized mass demonstrations, eliminated or abducted businessmen, and killed officers and soldiers. They carried out reprisals against ORDEN members in the countryside and blew up barracks, banks, and newspaper offices. They laid ambushes for patrolling security forces and occupied government ministries, embassies, places of worship, and radio stations.

Romero had been informed weeks in advance about the planned coup of October 15, 1979. In the downfall of the general with the same surname, Romero saw "the end of the violence, the lies, and the corruption." On the night of October 15, he prepared a press release which was meant to avoid "any extremism whatsoever of the right or the left" in what he hoped would be a positive moment for the country. The communiqué asked the people to practice "patience" and called on the left to avoid "fanaticism." Those on the right were alarmed by the reformist manifesto of the coup leaders. Romero reminded them that instead of "unjustly defending one's own interests and economic, social, and political privileges," as they had done until then, they ought to show concern "for justice and for the voice of the poor, because this is the cause of the Lord himself who calls us to conversion and who one day will judge all humanity." The communiqué therefore expressed "conditional support" for the new government: the fulfillment of the proclamation issued by the coup leaders on October 15 was the real test.

Romero saw the political changes brought about on October 15, 1979, as a chance to avoid civil war. After years of hatred and appallingly bloody events, he felt that it was necessary not to waste the opportunity. He maintained that in those circumstances of national history everyone—from the worker to the businessman—had to collaborate: "We are all called to contribute our grain of sand at this hour of national rebuilding." In a document sent to the World Council of Churches, Romero went so far as to say about the Junta that "never before in the history of our nation has a government given so much hope to the country."

To Romero's surprise, however, the country seemed to rush headlong into increased violence. It was provoked both by the right-wing military and by the guerrilla groups supported by popular organizations. The reformist solution infuriated both the proponents of the status quo and those of the revolution. Romero began again, in his homilies, to speak out against the violence. He condemned the bloodshed perpetrated by the security forces. Two demonstrations, on October 29 and 31, 1979, concluded with a total of eighty dead and hundreds of civilians wounded. Romero remarked: "Maybe the security forces are using brutal means of repression, more brutal than in the previous regime, because they are trying to keep this new government from earning credibility...." But it had its share of the blame:

> The Junta has tried to justify the massacre, arguing that the government responded to the demonstrators' aggression with an exercise of the citizens' right to legitimate defense, as a way of protecting the many who might have been innocent victims.... One of the conditions for a legitimate defense ... is that the defensive action be proportionate to the action of the unjust aggressor. If someone comes unarmed to hurt me with his bare hands, I must not respond with weapons.... Even if there were provocations, in no way can a defense that left such a massacre after a demonstration be proportionate. The warlike means that were utilized and the results make it clear that this moral principle was violated on that occasion.

Romero again did not neglect to denounce any violence whatsoever committed by the armed leftists too: in one week, eight members of the security forces were killed in different ambushes and attacks, and another week saw "the summary execution committed vindictively" of eleven farmers accused of collaborating with ORDEN. Taking his cue from the latter incident, which occurred in the vicinity of San Pedro Perulapán, the scene of a massacre carried out by the military one year before, Romero declared on Christmas Eve 1979:

> I want to address now, with the same pastoral urgency, the popular groups and their armed forces, which have committed a series of acts that left many families in mourning and spread destruction and fear in the country. I mean the massacres of many individuals simply because it was thought that they belonged to ORDEN or were collaborators with the previous regime. . . . Inhabitants of several cantons point out the

dangerous imprudence of publishing lists that threaten people who very often are innocent. In any case, no one can take revenge on his own authority.

Amid acts of brutality committed by both sides, Romero attempted to keep some hope alive. To this end he became personally involved, exhausting himself in mediation between the parties. He dialogued with everyone, and tried to resolve risky situations. One example was the time when he stood between a group of demonstrators who had shut themselves up in a church with a National Guardsman as hostage, and detachments of that same Guard that had surrounded the church and intended to attack it. Romero's mediation succeeded. The hostage was set free and a slaughter was avoided. Many times Romero intervened to petition the Junta to approve the expected agrarian reform: "The Junta does not have the right but the obligation to transform agriculture." In his homilies he listed the problems in the rural areas, citing official statistics:

> Sixty-seven percent of *campesino* mothers give birth without any medical assistance. Sixty out of every thousand babies born in the countryside die. Only thirty-seven percent of rural families have access to sources of water. Seventy-three percent of peasant children are undernourished. Fifty percent of the rural population cannot read. More than 250,000 rural families live in lodgings with only one room, whereas the average family has 5.6 members. This scandalous situation that our *campesino* brethren are enduring is explained to a great extent if you take into account the unjust and disproportionate distribution of land. . . . Ninety-nine percent of the landowners possess scarcely 51 percent of all the land. This means that almost all of them divide half of El Salvador among themselves; on the other hand not even 1 percent, a mere 0.7 percent of the landowners possess 40 percent of the land. And this is better quality land.

By late December 1979, Romero knew of the political attrition of the Junta, but he asked people to keep hoping, since he saw no alternative but chaos. He pointed out positive steps the Junta had taken: laws preventing the press from slandering anonymously, measures against usury, a rent freeze, and improvement of hygiene in the urban shanty-towns (*"los Tugurios"*). Nevertheless the violence did not decrease. The military carried out assassinations. ORDEN acted under other guises. The news about the *desaparecidos* promised by the executive branch did not arrive. There were no deliberations on agrarian reform. Foreign trade in coffee, sugar, and cotton was not nationalized as had been promised initially. The interests of the oligarchy were not debated, and therefore neither was the situation of social injustice. The Junta was increasingly divided between its military and civilian components. These difficulties were reflected in the sorrowful notes in Romero's speeches. On December 23, 1979, he preached, not knowing that the days of the Junta were already numbered:

> In the light of this message of Christmas, we see on our national scene a contrast on the one hand between death, hatred, revenge, blood, violence, and suffering, and on the other hand a few faint rays of hope. So let us be like the Messiah, about whom Isaiah said: "A bruised reed he will not break, and a dimly burning wick he will not quench." As true followers of Jesus, let us revive hope wherever it may be found and let us also denounce the sowing of evil wherever it occurs.

In his homily on December 31, 1979, he offered a religious response to the uncertainties of national life:

> We are living in very uncertain times. What awaits us in 1980? Will it be the year of civil war? Will it be the year of total destruction? Will we have merited God's mercy because of the great

amount of blood that has already been shed—and shed with
hatred, repression, and violence? As we face this uncertain future,
may the Lord have mercy on us. I do not want to be pessimistic,
because I want to tell you that the power of prayer sustains us. . . .
As this year ends, given the prospects of sorrow, suffering, and
uncertainty in human time, let us lift our sights to God's eternity.
We will see the coming of his blessing, his Son, his forgiveness. . . .
We have traveled over only a small stretch of the great pilgrimage
of history. . . . There in heaven the continuous passage of time
does not exist. Time is an imperfection, time is transitory; eternity is the everlasting present.

Since mid-October Romero had been harshly criticized by the
faction on the left that could not identify with the Junta. The prevailing mindset, on the left as on the right, left no room for nuances
and arbitration. Neutral positions were rejected. This was the tragedy of the so-called *evolucionados* [i.e., those whose thinking is
"developed" or advanced]. Romero's stance made him one; in June
1979 he had told a Costa Rican newspaper: "The extreme left and
the extreme right, for different reasons, are both trying to destroy
rational forums and any seeds whatsoever of openness to democracy. This explains why those who are most clearly *evolucionados*
have been hit all the more by both factions." The journalist who had
interviewed him commented:

> This is obvious. In El Salvador if you want to die quickly, just
> show that you are democratic, conciliatory, civilized. If you are an
> extremist you have many more opportunities to survive. . . . Both
> the extreme left and the extreme right, albeit for different reasons,
> drown in blood any gleam of hope for progress. The former are
> interested in bringing about a universal crisis, the best point of
> departure for rebellion and revolution. For the extreme right it is
> unthinkable that their medieval privileges could disappear, and
> they share the notion that anyone who claims to change the status
> quo is liable to death.

After the October 15 coup, the left stirred up anger that Romero was not using his moral authority against the new government. His request to be patient and not to obstruct the work of the Junta disappointed those who saw the overthrow of the government as an attempt to avoid execution by revolution. Romero, who had received so many death threats from the right, received some from the left too. In guerrilla circles, documents were circulating that spoke about him as a "traitor." Romero ironically remarked: "Some used to treat me as a Communist; now, in contrast, others consider me a traitor." He responded to the critiques of those whom he described as "opposition leaders by profession, prejudice, or political position," inviting them to "understand the agility of history": "Let us learn to speak the language of politics and not just the language of violence. Let us be flexible in redefining our analysis and our agendas, when they no longer correspond to reality. History is not constrained by rigid systems. . . . The important thing today, more than ever, is the good of the fatherland, not the good of your own organization."

For Romero, flexibility meant adopting constructive attitudes. Life was not only a struggle; it was also common work and mutual collaboration. The extreme left insisted exclusively on the *lucha*, the struggle, and Romero ironically mused: "We are not against the *lucha prolongada*. We have had an even more prolonged struggle: for twenty centuries we have been struggling against all tyrannies and all sorts of slavery, but in the name of him who does not conform to any specific worldly plan." Romero was sure that he had not deviated from a consistent line of defending human rights, justice, the poor, and the people. He declared in the cathedral in December 1979:

> Why does this society need to have farmers without work, poorly paid laborers, and people without a fair wage? These mechanisms

must be discovered, not as someone studies sociology or economy, but as Christians, so as not to be complicit. . . . The Church supports everyone who promotes structural change. She does not stop at that, of course, because she said in the voice of Paul VI: "To change structures without changing the hearts of men is simply to place the new structures at the service of new sins." "What is needed is a new man," Medellín said. "And in order to have a new continent, it is not enough to have a change of structure without a change of hearts." This, dear brothers and sisters, is my aim as pastor! Here I am not defending one economic system or the other. . . . I am trying to shed light on any economic system that is in keeping with the Lord's word of justice. And I require of all systems, of all parties, of all organizations, of all who truly love the good of their country, that they convert! And from the perspective of a Gospel conversion they ought to give people the remedy that these people need.

In those crucial months, Romero had plenty of grief from his own milieu. The most radicalized sectors of the Salvadoran Church challenged him. Romero was accused by some priests from "*la Nacional*" of having "sold out" to the military government. A group of priests, religious, and lay people from all over the country anonymously circulated a manifesto denouncing Romero's conduct: the archbishop purportedly had betrayed the people by supporting the Junta of the military leaders of the coup. Romero grieved especially because the document showed that the mindset of the local Church was more political than religious.

Toward Civil War

On January 2, 1980, the civilian members of the Junta submitted their resignations, after one last conflict with the right-wing military. An agreement signed on January 9 between the armed forces and the Christian Democratic Party led to a new Revolutionary Government, of which Duarte was now a part. The internal dialectic of the second Junta was almost the same as that of the first: on the one hand were those who attempted structural reforms, and on the other hand were those who just wanted to put down the revolutionary insurgency. The objective of the right-wing military was to root out violently any leftist forces. The left responded to the violence of the right with its own. In the months of January and February 1980 almost 600 persons died because of political violence. Military repression caused most of the victims. El Salvador embarked on the psychosis of declared civil war. Unlike the first Revolutionary Government, the second Junta did not have the benefit of the hopes raised by the coup. The context seemed unfavorable, even though the Christian Democratic Party, which was its pillar on the civilian side, had a following in the country. The right-wing military was better organized and controlled crucial public operations. It was the time to set aside any democratic scruple. Constitutional safeguards, which had previously been disparaged by the military and the oligarchy, were definitively replaced by the ideology of national security—the same ideology about which the Argentine General Saint-Jean had declared three years earlier: "First we kill all the subversives, then their collaborators, then the indifferent, and last of all the timid." Meanwhile the various guerrilla groups were unifying in one revolutionary front.

The two extreme factions sought to radicalize the clash. Terror increased in the countryside. At night the farmers preferred to sleep outdoors. It made little difference whether regular armed detachments or clandestine death squads conducted the campaign of repression. People everywhere were disappearing. Corpses turned up here and there with the typical horrendous mutilations designed to terrify. More than once, machine guns were used to end strikes. The guerrillas, in turn, did not hesitate to pursue a strategy of increasing the tension with more bloodshed, abductions, and the destruction of property. To stir up a populace that otherwise would have preferred to settle their political problems peacefully, the guerrillas needed brutal and indiscriminate repression: the deaths of many innocent people, setting fire to the fields, thousands of evacuees, and growing popular resentment. A psychological escalation of terror took place. Both sides drew up lists of persons to terrify and strike down. Any concern about disguising the illegality of these campaigns ceased.

During the last months of his life, Romero was tormented by the spread of repression and violence. The images of blood and death saddened him unspeakably. His role was by no means played out. As the situation in the country glowed white-hot, Romero immersed himself in the national crisis. He maintained frequent contacts with all sides: the military, Christian Democrats, opposition leaders, politicians of various stripes, diplomats, businessmen, intellectuals. As a matter of principle he also encouraged the new Junta in its program of social justice, citing the proclamation on October 15, 1979. Nevertheless, he did not place in it the confidence that he had had in the preceding Junta. He still disputed the idea that repression should take priority over reforms. At the same time he emphasized his denunciation of the power that the military exercised in parallel with the Junta. He also attacked the oligarchy, inasmuch as it pursued a strategy of opposing reforms, even if it cost the destruction of the country. He asked the popular organizations to contribute responsibly toward solving the national crisis in the name of the common good, while distancing themselves from violence. He resolutely condemned guerrilla warfare. Day after day, Romero became more skeptical about the practical options of what still emphatically described itself as the Revolutionary Government. Romero ended up saying that it was a ridiculous title.

Several times during those months Romero used the schema of "the three plans" or "the three options" that existed in Salvadoran politics. These were the respective plans of the oligarchy, the government, and the popular organizations. Romero did not adopt any of these three plans, but every week he updated his judgment on them, based on the situation in the country. Romero judged on the basis of only one principle: for the Church "what matters in the various political situations are the poor people." "The world of the poor" was in the socio-political field "the ultimate theological and historical criterion for the Church's conduct": "Depending on how things go for them, for the poor people, the Church will support, in the proper way as Church, one or another political plan."

According to Romero, the oligarchy's plan was marked by its strenuous defense of its own interests: power and wealth. Since this was incompatible with the common good, it was unacceptable. The archbishop's invitation to the oligarchs was summed up in the verb *compartir.* That is, they should *share* their goods and privileges before it was too late, before civil war broke out and violently carried off all their wealth. As for the other two plans, Romero neither promoted nor rejected them in their entirety but distinguished between "the sound part that exists in each and the unsound, inhumane, anti-Christian part that is also found in each." Thus Romero summed up "the three plans: the Church rejects the plan of the right, while she asks [the faithful] to collaborate with the sound part of the other two and to cut away the part that is unsound."

Romero asked the government to stop the repression and to implement reforms. The executive branch must punish those guilty of repressive abuses, compensate the victims, and explain what happened to the *desaparecidos.* On March 5, 1980, the eve of the promulgation of the agrarian reform law, Romero informed the Junta that the law met with his consent. Yet the Church could not "feel fully confident" in the government while the reforms were accompanied by the "massacre of the people." The "repressive nature" of the government's action was "offensive to the people." And so, the archbishop maintained his friendship with various members of the government at "a personal level only." In any case Romero repeated his proposal to give "my favorable judgment on all the positive things that should be supported, while also expressing my reservations, always with the good of the people in view." From the pulpit, Romero was more radical. He deemed it "impossible" for a government "to promote processes and plans for reforms and social changes while at the same time a climate of repression persists." Hidden amid the reforms was "the torrent of the people's blood that is being shed." On March 14 Romero spent the evening with Colonel Majano and the Christian Democrat Morales Ehrlich. Both were members of the Junta. Given the "hope" and the "joy" of the two men because of the launch of the agrarian reform and other anti-oligarchic means, Romero at first congratulated them. Then he expressed his doubts: "I primarily pointed out . . . how the agrarian reform is connected to this visible wave of violent repression by the security forces. This takes credibility away from the agrarian reform and lacks the support of the people."

According to Romero, given the prospect of a return to democracy, the Junta needed to consider the place of the popular organizations. They would have to free themselves, however, from the negative elements they still had. Romero's critiques of the popular organizations were not new, but somehow they were more heartfelt and intense. It was urgent that they "should break with sectarian and partisan interests." In particular they had to respect the religious sentiments of the majority of the people; indeed they ought to value them: "without prayer there can be no redemption." Romero said: "The claims of the people are quite just, and we have to keep defending social justice and love for the poor . . . but precisely for this reason: if we truly love the people and are trying to defend them, let us not take away from them what is most valuable—their faith in God." Most importantly, the popular organizations had to renounce violence. On this point Romero was categorical: "Violence is a regression of civilization; it is the expression of man's primitive character." The "irrational combativeness" had to stop. "As for the popular plan, I wish to tell you the same thing that I say about the government's plan: that words and promises are not enough, especially when they are shouted frantically in a demagogic spirit. Deeds are needed. . . . Let these often senseless acts of violence and terrorism cease now, for they provoke even more violent situations." Eight days before being killed, Romero concluded his Sunday homily by turning "to those who support violent solutions": "I wish to call them to understanding. May they know that nothing violent can be lasting. There are also human prospects of reasonable solutions and, especially, above all, there is the word of God that has cried out to us today: Reconciliation!"

Romero did not give himself up to any political force. He supported solutions, not factions. The reality was complex and especially confused. The Salvadoran tragedy had many different actors. Romero sought to stay in contact with them all. He had an appointment to meet with the leaders of the Christian Democratic Party on the day after his assassination. In the preceding days he had had contacts with the directors of the popular organizations. In his homilies Romero continually recalled that "it is not the Church's job to identify herself with one plan or another, nor to be the leader of an eminently political process."

The Church's tremendous role is to sustain in human history the plan of God's history. It is to reflect this history of God in people's everyday lives, so as to approve everything that reflects God's plan of salvation in history. Also, with the sacred freedom of God, it is to reject in human history anything that does not correspond to the plan, the design of God who wants to save humanity. Therefore the Church must not identify herself with historical human plans but rather must enlighten them all.

Romero's last public statements deal not so much with political arguments as with his protest against the spread of repression and violence. He preached on March 16, 1980:

> Once again the Lord asks Cain: Where is Abel, your brother? And although Cain answers the Lord that he is not his brother's keeper, the Lord replies: "The voice of your brother's blood is crying to me from the ground. And now you are cursed from the ground, which has opened its mouth to receive your brother's blood from your hand. When you till the ground, it shall no longer yield to you its strength." . . . Nothing is as important to the Church as human life, the human person—above all, the persons of the poor and the oppressed. They are not only human beings but also divine beings, because everything that is done to them, Jesus said, he takes as being done to him. And that blood, all bloodshed or death, goes beyond any sort of politics and touches the very heart of God. . . . Let us not forget those words of God to Cain: the bloodied ground will never again be productive.

Romero's Lent

Romero was tormented by what was happening. He was obsessed by the blood that was shed in the repression. That blood made so many innocent victims—among them women, children, unarmed people, his own friends. He also condemned the violence of guerrilla warfare but was convinced that it would be appeased once a democratic government had removed the situation of social injustice that existed in the country. Romero's continuous public interventions between January and March 1980 were dictated more by pity over the ongoing *matanza* [slaughter] than by any sort of *Realpolitik*. Besides, in that chaos, what did political realism mean? It meant to take sides, as almost everyone was doing. People sided either with the military repression and the oligarchy, or with the declared revolution. Only Romero proposed a genuine third alternative in the name of the teaching of the Gospel. As he kept repeating: "I would like to be at all times, especially in these hours of confusion, psychosis, and collective anxieties, a messenger of hope and joy, and there is reason for it. . . . Above and beyond the tragedies, the bloodshed, and the violence, there is a word of faith and hope that tells us: there is a way out, there is hope, we can rebuild our country. We Christians bring a unique power. Let us use it!" This smacked of utopian thinking, but the Christian, he said, believes in miracles. Romero did not doubt that El Salvador could be saved, provided that it had faith. He preached about the wedding feast at Cana:

> It will seem paradoxical to some that we should be invited to joy when El Salvador is in such great affliction, such great fear, such great madness. Yet no appeal is more relevant to our fatherland and to Salvadorans than this morning's liturgical appeal, which calls us to gladness and optimism. . . . Mary's anxiety expresses humanity's anxiety: "They have no more wine." We can apply this sentence to many human needs: We have no bread! The country is on the wrong track! Anxieties on every side! Violence! Disorder! And nevertheless the anxiety is brimming with hope, as is the case with Mary. She senses that her Son is the powerful one who can solve problems that humanly speaking cannot be solved. For her it is enough to say to him: "They have no more wine," to present the need to him with the confidence of faith which knows that the miracle must come about. Ah! If only we Salvadorans

knew how to tell Jesus about the anxiety of this hour with Mary's confidence, without pessimism and desperation. . . .

According to Romero, Christianity was superior to politics. The solution to El Salvador's crisis lay not in the victory of one party or the other, but in the triumph of a Christian vision of the human person. Respect for the human person was needed first of all. Therefore Romero asked those on the right to make a commitment to *compartir*,[2] and those on the left to give up ideologies that debased human dignity. In the above-cited homily from the day before he died, Romero denounced

> . . . the false visions of the world that people have created for their own interests, especially those that make the person an instrument to exploit, or those Marxist ideologies that make the person nothing more than a cog in a machine, or [the ideologies] that make the National Security forces a servant of the State, as though the State were the master and people were the slaves, whereas, on the contrary, the person was not made for the State but the State for the person. The person must be at the summit of every human organization. . . . This is the basis for our sociology, which we have learned from Christ in his Gospel.

Romero made every effort to avoid the worst. He tried to mediate, to bring opposing sides closer together, to reconcile, to find solutions based on justice. On March 16, 1980, he preached:

> There is a lot of violence, a lot of hatred, a lot of egotism. Everyone thinks that he has the truth and blames the other for the evils. . . . Without being aware of it, each one of us is polarized, stubbornly takes one side. We are incapable of reconciliation; we hate to the

---

2. This is translated, "to share." —*Ed.*

death. This is not the environment that God wants. It is an environment that needs God's great love more than ever and that allows reconciliation. . . . How much we here in El Salvador need to meditate a bit on this parable of the prodigal son! How irreconcilable they seem, the left's denunciation of the right and the right's hatred of the left, while those in the middle say: "Let the violence come from wherever it may come from; it is cruel in either case." And so we live in polarized groups, and those in the same group may not even love one another because there can be no love where there is so much partisanship that people hate each other. We need to break these barriers and to realize that there is a father who loves us all and is waiting for us all. We need to learn to recite the Our Father and to say to him: "Forgive us, as we forgive." This is reconciliation. . . .

Death

Romero had received insults and threats in his first year as archbishop of San Salvador, mostly through anonymous letters. Then the telephone calls began, day and night. Now and then the faithful reported to him threatening opinions that they had heard in circles hostile to him. Thus in 1978 he was informed that "the rich in that area [Santa Ana] are very annoyed at *Monseñor* and criticize his preaching, describing him as a Communist, and [they say] that the best solution for the government would be to have him killed." "Rumors" about his imminent assassination (as Romero had previously described them, as though to diminish their significance) had proliferated in 1979. Even the formidable *Unión Guerrera Blanca* had warned him. From co-workers he received transcripts of telephone calls between directors of the secret military police in which they discussed possible attempts on the archbishop's life. As of

October 1979, the death threats from the right were joined by those from the left, because of Romero's support for the Revolutionary Government. At the end of 1979 Romero no longer thought that the threats were rumors. He knew that he could die at any moment and wondered whether the right or the left would kill him. During his spiritual exercises in Planes de Renderos in late February 1980, he explained to his confessor,[3] Father Azcue, that he had two fears: one concerned distraction in the spiritual and ascetical life; the other had to do with "the risks to my own life. It's hard for me to accept the idea of a violent death, which in these circumstances is very possible." But he added confidently: "I will cope with unknown circumstances with God's grace. He assisted the martyrs, and if it is necessary I will feel that he is very close as I offer him my last breath. But what matters more than the moment of death is to give him my whole life and to live for him." To Azcue, the archbishop appeared "terrified, like Jesus in the Garden of Olives." Yet during that same retreat Romero wrote in his notes:

> In this way I, too, place under his loving providence all my life, and I accept my death, no matter how difficult it may be, with faith in him. I will not offer a prayer intention, as I would like to, for peace in my country or for the flourishing of our Church . . . because the Heart of Christ will know best how to work things to the destiny he desires. It is enough for me to be happy and confident, knowing with certainty that my life and my death are in his hands and that, despite my sins, I have put my trust in him and I will not be disappointed. Others, with more wisdom and holiness, will carry on the works of the Church and of the nation.

---

3. As recounted by Romero in his retreat notes. —*Ed.*

These are deeply-meditated words of a man who foresaw his imminent death. Yet he had no intention of fleeing from the responsibilities that inexorably led him to that death. Remarkably, Romero gave a purely religious meaning to the death he expected.

In his final months Romero experienced the death threats with intermittent anguish. His agitation did not show when he was preaching or conducting official business, but in his private life Romero alternated between serenity and depression. He experienced mood swings and sudden attacks of anxiety. During the afore-mentioned retreat in Planes de Renderos he got up at night to go over and sleep in the common dormitory. He courteously apologized: "I was afraid. I spent the whole night thinking that a bullet could have come through the door or the windows." When he slept in his residence at the *Hospitalito* he used to wake up suddenly because of the avocados that sometimes fell on the roof, mistaking them for a shot or a bomb aimed at him. Out of caution, in his final days he slept on a cot in the sacristy of the church of the *Hospitalito*, the same church where he would be killed. Today, a wall surrounds the property of the Hospital of Divine Providence, including the small guard house at its edge, where Romero lived. But in 1980 it was an open space. Romero's fear was justified.

Meanwhile, many advised Romero to take precautions. The government offered escorts and armored cars. The Holy See offered him temporary hospitality in Rome. An alarming incident occurred in early February. D'Aubuisson, who by then had moved on to organizing death squads, read on television a list of two hundred individuals infected by Communism and involved with guerrilla warfare. Among them was Romero, about whom D'Aubuisson said that "there was still time for him to correct his errors." This death threat, even if not immediate, was to be taken seriously. In El Salvador the terrorist organization on the right liked to give macabre warnings to their future victims. On March 9, there was a failed attack in the Basilica of the Sacred Heart that Romero used instead of the cathedral, which was occupied by leftist organizations. Although the attack caused no harm, it was extremely serious. A suitcase containing seventy-two sticks of dynamite was placed beside a pillar supporting the cupola. It had been set to explode during a Mass for the repose of the soul of Mario Zamora, a Christian Democratic leader who had been assassinated shortly before. Romero was celebrating Mass and the entire leadership of the Christian Democratic Party was present. Had it not been for the defective timer, the explosion would have been enough to destroy the basilica and perhaps the entire block of buildings. The police munitions experts thought that in the event of an explosion all those attending the Mass would have died. The explosion was not of the sort used by the guerrillas.

Although convinced that he was in serious danger, Romero chose not to hire protection, so as not to involve anyone else in a possible attack on his person. He traveled about alone in an automobile. On March 14 he told the ambassador from the United States: "I only hope that when they kill me, they do not kill many of us." He did not want to have more protection than the unarmed people who suffered because of the bloody incursions of the security forces and death squads: "Pastorally, it would be a negative witness if I traveled about in safety while my people were living in danger." He told a journalist on March 15: "My duty obliges me to walk with my people; it would not be right to give a witness of fear. If death comes, it will be the moment to die as God willed." Although many were suggesting he should go abroad, his decision not to do so but to remain at his post seemed necessary to him since he was a bishop, who does not abandon his faithful. As early as December 1978,

Bishop Quarracino had warned him about the danger of a violent death. Romero had commented: "A pastor does not go away; he must stay to the end with his own." In May 1977, after the assassination of one of his priests, he had said:

> The Second Vatican Council says that not all will have the honor of physically giving their blood, of being killed for the faith. But God asks of all who believe in him a spirit of martyrdom. In other words, we all must be ready to die for our faith, even if the Lord does not grant us that honor. We indeed are willing, so that, when our hour arrives to give him an accounting, we can say: "Lord, I was ready to give my life for you. And I gave it." Because to give one's life does not only mean to be killed. To give one's life, to have the spirit of martyrdom is to give in performing one's duties, in silence and prayer, in fulfilling one's responsibilities honestly. It is to give one's life little by little, in the silence of everyday life, as a mother gives who, without fear, with the simplicity of maternal martyrdom, gives birth to her child and nurses him, raises him, and affectionately looks after him.

Two years later, martyrdom was a familiar theme for the archbishop. He noted during his visit to Rome in May 1979:

> This morning I went again to Saint Peter's Basilica. There, before the altars that I love so much of Saint Peter and his more recent successors, I have asked with insistence for the gift of fidelity to my Christian faith and for the courage, if necessary, either to die as all these martyrs did or to live consecrating my life in the same way that these modern day successors of Peter have done.

Romero was not pursuing a heroic course of action. The poor of El Salvador, to whom he compared his own life, were not heroes but oppressed people who longed for better days. Romero's dream was not that of a fearless champion but of a simple man: an end to the violence and destruction; justice in Salvadoran society; the opportunity for all to live in peace and tranquility; freedom for the Church to proclaim the Gospel and to reconcile. Romero fostered an ideal of honest, hard-working, religious, humble life. So he preached even as the civil war was already looming:

> There is no greater joy than to earn one's bread by the sweat of one's brow. . . . God's plan is the simplicity of the man of faith, living his ordinary life, who wins God's favor and draws near to God. There is no need to do showy things. . . . This is God's plan: simple, ordinary life, but with a feeling of love and freedom. How beautiful our country would be if we all lived according to this plan of God! Each one busy with his occupation, without any pretense of dominating, simply earning a living and eating in justice the bread that his family needs.

The terrible pressure of current events was not easy to bear. In the last months of his life Romero increased the amount of time that he dedicated to prayer and to meditation before the Blessed Sacrament. His favorite psalm, significantly, was Psalm 91, a hymn of assurance of God's protection.

On March 24, 1980, Monday of the last week of Lent, Romero was killed during an afternoon Mass for the repose of the soul of Sara de Pinto, an acquaintance of his. The day before he had said in his Sunday homily:

> Just as [Christ] will flourish in an unending Easter, we must accompany him in a Lent and a Holy Week that means cross, sacrifice, martyrdom, or as he said, "Blessed are they who are not scandalized by his cross!" Lent, then, is a call to celebrate our redemption in that difficult compound of cross and victory. Our people are very prepared, everything around us preaches the cross; but those who have Christian faith and hope know that behind this calvary of El Salvador is our Easter, our resurrection, and that is the hope of the Christian people.

The homily had lasted about two hours. Romero had made his famous appeal to the soldiers not to obey orders contrary to God's law and not to kill:

> I would like to make a very special appeal to the men of the army . . . before a man's order to kill, God's law, which says, "Do not kill," must prevail. No soldier is obliged to obey an order that goes against God's law. . . . The Church, defender of the rights of God, of the law of God, of the dignity of the human person, cannot remain silent in the face of such abominations. . . . In the name of God, then, and in the name of this suffering nation, whose increasingly tumultuous cries rise to heaven, I beg you, I plead with you, I command you in the name of God: Stop the repression!

The high military command regarded such an appeal as a gravely subversive act. Hypothetically, if he had been subject to military regulations, Romero could have been found guilty of inciting insubordination and punished with execution by a firing squad. Probably the archbishop's assassination, which had been planned for some time, was precipitated by that appeal. On Monday morning the perpetrators of the crime found in the major newspapers of San Salvador a notice about the Mass that Romero would celebrate at five thirty that afternoon, for the repose of the soul of Sara de Pinto, and they decided to take action.

But let us stay with the events of Sunday. In the late morning, after Mass, Romero dined at the Barrazas' house. It was now one o'clock. At the Barraza house, Romero played with the children. At table, however, he seemed bewildered:

> He took off his glasses, something he never did, and remained in a silence that was very striking to all of us. He was visibly dejected and sad. He ate his soup slowly and looked attentively at us one by

one. Eugenia, my wife, who was sitting beside him at the table, was perturbed by a long, profound look that he gave her, as though he wanted to tell her something. Tears streamed from his eyes. Lupita scolded him: "But why? What is there to cry about?" We were all perplexed. Suddenly he began to talk about his best friends, priests and laymen. He named them one by one, expressing admiration for each one of them and praising the virtues that he had noticed and the gifts that God had given them. In our house there had never been a lunch like that. It was sad and disconcerting for us all.

In the afternoon Salvador Barraza accompanied Romero to Calle Real, a little village almost at the periphery of San Salvador, to administer first Holy Communion and Confirmation to many youngsters. In the car Romero played marimba music, his favorite. In the little village church, performing his pastoral duties among affectionate people, he regained his vitality. He was cordial and attentive with everyone. On the return trip, as they neared the Barrazas' house, he went back to being gloomy. He started to watch the circus on television. The clowns usually amused him, but this time they saddened him. They were showing the story of an old clown, and Romero said that when you get old "you are no longer in fashion and you are not good for anything." It was very sad.

On Monday Romero went in the early morning, as always, to the church of the *Hospitalito* to pray. He was wearing white clothing, which meant that he was going to the ocean. The sisters pretended that they wanted to go too, and Romero jokingly cited a verse from the Gospel of John: "Where I am going you cannot come." He stopped briefly at the diocesan chancery and then went to the ocean with other priests from Opus Dei. This was one of Romero's periodic retreats with Opus Dei, which were moments of rest, study, and priestly fellowship. Their destination was the beach of La Libertad, a half-hour journey from San Salvador. Because of a misunderstanding with the custodian, when they arrived at the house on the ocean with its palm garden, they found it closed. Some of them, including Romero, scaled the enclosing wall and opened the gate for the others. The place was enchanting and silent. They studied a recent Vatican document on priestly formation that Romero had brought. They spoke also about material assistance for the seminary and the sacred furnishings of the cathedral. Romero was worried that the occupations of the cathedral might cause damage or fire and asked Sáenz Lacalle to take anything precious that was there into temporary custody. Since he had a slight ear infection, Romero did not go swimming in the warm waters of the Pacific. They ate while sitting on the lawn. In the afternoon Romero returned to the city and went to see a doctor about his ear. Then he went to Santa Tecla to make a brief confession to Father Azcue. Barraza accompanied him, and in the car they talked about a platform to be set up for the solemn liturgy on Palm Sunday, the following Sunday. At 5:30 PM he returned to the *Hospitalito* for the Mass for the repose of the soul of Sara de Pinto, which started late.

The homily in memory of *Doña Sarita*, as Romero called her, contained nothing unusual. It was a Mass celebrated in a familiar style, in the modest church of the *Hospitalito* where Romero lived. Several terminally ill patients also attended. Romero praised the deceased woman for having spent her life for her neighbor. He developed the theme of life in heaven, in which *Doña Sarita*, like all who had lived in Christian hope, would find "purified," "illuminated," and "transfigured" anything good that they had done on earth. He concluded the homily:

> This Eucharist is really an act of faith. With Christian faith we know that in this moment the host made of wheat is changed into the Body of the Lord who offered himself for the redemption of the world, and that in the chalice, wine is transformed into the

Blood that was the price of salvation. May this Body that is immolated and this Blood which is sacrificed for men, also nourish us so that we can give over our body and our blood to suffering and pain, as Christ did, not for ourselves, but rather so as to bring forth a harvest of justice and peace in our land. Let us unite together intimately then in faith and hope during this moment of prayer for *Doña Sarita* and for ourselves.

This was Romero's *amen*. He had spoken in front of the altar. Then he turned to take the corporal with which to begin the offertory. At that moment a gunshot came from one of the entrances to the church. Romero fell beside the altar. The faithful, frightened, threw themselves down on the ground for a few seconds. When they stood up again, they saw that Romero was still prostrate, and they approached to help him. Romero was losing blood, did not move, and seemed to be unconscious. The bullet had fragmented. It had not struck vital organs but had exploded in his chest. Romero was loaded onto a truck and brought to the *Policlínica Salvadoreña*, where shortly after his arrival he died of internal bleeding. He was sixty-two years old.

On March 30, Palm Sunday, Romero's funeral Mass began but was not completed. A large crowd had gathered on the Plaza Barrios in front of the cathedral. During the ceremony one bomb or more exploded on the plaza. Shooting began and panic broke out. Several dozen persons died. While the funeral was descending into chaos, the bier with Romero's body was carried from the square into the cathedral, where arrangements were made hastily to entomb the archbishop's remains. Immediately, different versions and interpretations of the incident began to circulate, none of which was incontrovertible in light of the available evidence and testimonies. In all probability, the chaos started with the explosion of a paper bomb, a large but harmless noisemaker that causes no casualties.

Armed leftist militants began shooting frantically, and perhaps members of the military, hidden within the surrounding mansions, also began shooting. Nevertheless, the casualties were almost all caused by the terror that seized the crowd; in the panicked rush to flee, many were trampled and crushed. Probably the full truth about Romero's interrupted funeral will never be known. John Rafael Quinn, Archbishop of San Francisco, who participated in Romero's funeral, commented as follows on the mutual accusations of responsibility for the incidents: "The question is not who is to blame but, on the contrary, who is more to blame."

Amid great difficulties Judge Atilio Ramírez Amaya began investigations into the murder of Romero. Police agencies began their work several days later. The persons present at Romero's last Mass were not brought in for questioning. The work of the technical experts was incomplete. While the investigations struggled, the assassins continued their operations. Several of the witnesses of the crime were killed or disappeared. Judge Ramírez was determined to work scrupulously on the case. An attempt on his life was made while he was at home on March 27, 1980, three days after Romero's death. Two armed men entered the house under some pretext and tried to assassinate him, but they didn't succeed because Ramírez was armed and defended himself. The judge decided then to flee to Venezuela. From there he accused Roberto D'Aubuisson of having organized the assassination of Romero. The murder investigations continued intermittently. They dragged on for fourteen years and never went to trial. There was no intention to do so during the civil war, which lasted from 1980 to 1992. After the peace agreements signed on January 16, 1992, a Commission on the Truth for El Salvador was established under the aegis of the United Nations. It was composed of international figures and legal experts, in order to shed light on the origins of the violence and on who was responsible for the crimes committed in El Salvador between January 1980 and July 1981. The final report of the Commission was presented to the Secretary General of the United Nations and to the public on March 15, 1993. It dealt extensively with the Romero case.

The report declared: "Former Major Roberto D'Aubuisson gave the order to assassinate the archbishop and gave precise instructions to members of his security detail, which was acting as a 'death squad,' to organize and supervise the assassination." The same D'Aubuisson later confidentially acknowledged "his intellectual authorship in the assassination of the archbishop of San Salvador." In reconstructing how the murder was carried out, the report of the Truth Commission says that the crime was committed by a group of four men in a red car, among them a professional killer who fired the one shot from outside the church. Three men from D'Aubuisson's entourage are said to have organized the logistics of Romero's murder, without personally participating in it. The report of the Truth Commission was based on various documents gathered in El Salvador, on unpublished testimonies, and on evidence derived from the incomplete files of the Salvadoran Justice Department.

The work of the Truth Commission could have given a decisive impetus in the Salvadoran courts to the judicial proceedings on Romero's murder, overcoming the investigative impasse. But the opposite happened. On March 20, 1993, only five days after the report was released, the Salvadoran Legislative Assembly approved a Law of General Amnesty for the Consolidation of the Peace, which granted "full, absolute, and unconditional amnesty to all persons who in any way have participated in the commission of political crimes" during the years of the civil war. All court-related activity regarding the killing of Romero was immediately suspended. The last dossier pertaining to it was formally sealed in 1994.

To this day the Salvadoran State, governed alternately by the right and the left, has not repealed the Amnesty Law in order to reopen investigations into Romero's assassination. Nevertheless, extra-judicially it has acknowledged that the report of the Truth Commission about the Romero case was true, and the State has admitted that its officials shared in responsibility for the archbishop's death. In the past twenty years various investigations by groups independent of any government, such as human rights associations, ecclesiastical commissions, investigative journals, as well as a California court, have substantially confirmed the results of the Truth Commission, which pointed to D'Aubuisson as the one who organized the murder. The thirty-six-year-old retired major had at his disposal in 1980 ample resources (money, houses, vehicles, staff) provided by members of the oligarchy for the campaigns of the death squads. He also had the active connivance of sectors of the army and of the security forces. Incidentally, D'Aubuisson smoked and drank very heavily and later died of a tumor in his throat in 1992, at the age of forty-eight. Although his military background had included training in the United States, he was opposed by the Americans because of his bloody excesses. The diplomats from the United States described him as a "psychopathic assassin" and stood in the way of his ambition to become president of El Salvador.

Conclusion

Romero did not change his deep convictions upon taking office as archbishop of San Salvador. Spiritually he remained firmly rooted in Tradition, the magisterium, and the Gospel. He had to confront a tragic situation, which brought to the fore his talents as a preacher and a public figure. Without Romero the conscientious priest, the man of prayer faithful to Rome and to Vatican II, Romero the passionate, charismatic archbishop probably would not have existed. Cardinal Roger Etchegaray wondered:

> Had he not made an effort to develop interiorly throughout his whole life, would he have agreed to sacrifice it? Had he not meditated countless times on Christ's passion, had he not prayed so much and so intensely before the crucifix, would he have remained at his post to the end? In 1956 Romero made a pilgrimage to the Holy Land: every evening, in Jerusalem, he went to pray in the Garden of Olives, until the middle of the night. Had he not

believed in the resurrection as he had always done, would he have resisted the threats that were so frequent in the last period of his life?

A popular biography of the militantly political sort makes a clear-cut distinction between Romero the archbishop and the earlier Romero. But he did not sense any discontinuity in his personal history. Romero never denied what he had believed since he was a boy. The references to persons and events of his past, in the writings and speeches of his final years, are still imbued with sentiment and emotion. During the night when he anxiously kept vigil beside the body of Rutilio Grande, he felt a call to change in the direction of a new *fortaleza*, not to break with his past as a conscientious ecclesiastic. Romero the archbishop experienced no conversion on the road to Damascus. He had a solid background of faith, doctrine, and piety. He had devoted himself very seriously to each duty entrusted to him, including that of archbishop of San Salvador. He had always been distinguished by his priestly integrity and ascetical rigor. He had a universal Catholic sensitivity, in a milieu that tended to concentrate on local issues. Rome was for him, until the end of his life, an essential point of reference.

Although Romero was a "Roman" priest and bishop, he was nevertheless not a "Western" bishop. This historical fact should be considered by those who thought that he took exaggerated positions against the public authorities, or by those who regarded his insistence on human rights as insufficiently ecclesiastical. El Salvador in the 1970s was ruled by a military regime that applied a local variation of the ideology of national security in favor of an oligarchy that was economically dynamic but politically reactionary. Although democracy was guaranteed in theory by the Constitution, it was denied in practice. A tacit agreement was in force in the ruling class, for whom any applicable laws were ignored in political life and in the labor marketplace. Elections were a sort of institutionalized fraud. The minimum wages guaranteed by law were not paid. Even the leader of the right-wing oligarchy later admitted the lack of justice and democracy in El Salvador at that time, such as to provoke well-founded reactions of protest. Alfredo Cristiani, President of El Salvador, acknowledged at the signing of the 1992 peace agreements that concluded the Salvadoran civil war:

> The crisis in Salvadoran society in the last decade did not come from nothing, nor was it the result of isolated purposes. This very sorrowful and tragic crisis has deep roots, ancient social, political, economic, and cultural roots. [These roots lie] in the complete lack or inadequacy of the forums and mechanisms necessary to allow for the free play of ideas, and the natural development of various political plans that result from freedom of thought and of action. In sum, the absence of a true democratic system of life.

Romero was not inspired by a fashionable political doctrine in opposing an unjust regime, that is, the dictatorship of the rich and of the military, which was the El Salvador of his day. It was not necessary to be a revolutionary to wish for the downfall of a government that showed contempt for the very Constitution and common law of the State. Romero's activity was founded on an ethical and religious view of reality. To his way of thinking, a political doctrine would not be enough for a true solution to the country's problems. Not even the Church's social doctrine would be enough. A true solution required the conversion of hearts.

Romero was a bishop in the bloody Latin America of his time. He was not a bishop in a country of the politically correct Western world. In this sense, Romero is difficult to understand in terms of Western categories. He was a bishop with a lofty sense of responsibility, who was deeply moved at the sight of bloodshed. He has been classified politically. But in order to be moved and to have compassion it was not necessary to be on the left or on the right. Romero was not a rationalist, nor was he a politician. Rather he was a man of intense feelings, a man of prayer who experienced history as a journey toward God.

Romero's beatification by the Catholic Church recognizes his martyrdom *in odium fidei*. Those who were his enemies during his lifetime thought that Romero had been killed out of hatred for his political positions. But it is difficult to argue that Romero, a bishop killed at the altar, during a Eucharistic liturgy, was not struck down *in odium fidei*, out of hatred for the faith. It was because of the faith that Romero spoke about reconciliation, loved the poor, and demanded social justice. It was because of the faith that he invited all to conversion and pointed out the sin of his contemporaries: this was the *kerygma*, the heart of the Gospel proclamation, as he used to say in his preaching. It was because of his confidence in the Gospel that Romero did not take cover from the threats, did not abandon his faithful, did not retreat, but accepted the death that he then knew was certain. Romero is a martyr for the Gospel, killed *in odium fidei*.

Romero's burial plaque quoted a love poem that began: "The kindest, meekest, most righteous, most handsome, noblest, holiest man has been killed." Romero had pronounced many eulogies, but he did not imagine that he would receive them *post mortem*. He did not feel holy. However in 1979 he had said, concerning some of his priests who had suffered a violent death: "What human being does not have something to repent of? The murdered priests were human beings too and had their sins. But the fact that they allowed their lives to be taken away without fleeing, without being cowards but accepting a sort of torture, suffering, assassination, in my opinion is precious as a baptism of blood, and they were purified. We must respect their memory." One could say the same about Romero's story and his martyrdom. People do not become martyrs because they are holy, but martyrdom purifies them.

No doubt Romero could have fled from death. He wanted to follow his conscience, understood in the Ignatian sense as the search for God's will. Romero's death was due to the fact that he was not resigned to the violence, the injustice, and the torment of his country. He felt that it was urgent to illuminate life with the Gospel. He had the charism of communicating in an extraordinary way with the crowds, translating the profound contents of Scripture into terms accessible to all. Like many martyrs before him, Romero was faithful to his mission. He did not flee.

The *odium*, the hatred toward Romero was real. Think of the many death threats, or of his systematic defamation in the extreme right-wing press. Since Romero spoke about social justice, he was accused of being Communist. He was ridiculed as "Marxnulfo," a play on his second name Arnulfo, although he had always maintained that Communism was an evil. In 1979, the year of Khomeini's triumph in Iran, they called him "the Salvadoran Ayatollah," so as to brand him as a fanatical agitator of the masses and an instigator of class hatred. This was *odium* for the way in which Romero lived the Gospel and for his being a bishop. Together with Romero, the Church was hated and persecuted, insofar as she called for justice, peace, and reconciliation. In order to be killed in the Salvadoran campaigns, it was enough to have a Bible, or to go to church to pray.

While the Catholic Church was involved in verifying the conditions for his canonization, the passionate disagreements about the figure of Romero raised the question of whether that process would be opportune. On May 9, 2007, Benedict XVI replied to a journalist who asked him for news about Romero's beatification process:

> Archbishop Romero was certainly an important witness of the faith, a man of great Christian virtue who worked for peace and

against the dictatorship, and was assassinated while celebrating Mass. Consequently, his death was truly "credible," a witness of faith. The problem was that a political party wrongly wished to use him as their banner, as an emblematic figure. How can we shed light on his person in the right way and protect it from these attempts to exploit it? This is the problem. It is under examination and I await confidently what the Congregation for the Causes of Saints will have to say on the matter.

A political myth has developed about Romero. It has not helped to overcome the prejudices of those who regarded him as a rabble-rouser, a subversive, a fanatic who became a media success. For a long time the glorification of Romero as a "martyr of the people," as the guerrillas styled him, imprisoned his figure in the stormy atmosphere of the Salvadoran civil war and the clash between right and left. It was already mentioned that Romero found himself being compared to Camilo Torres, "Che" Guevara, Salvador Allende and other "martyrs," if by martyrdom you mean dying while carrying a Tommy gun in the name of the people. The myth locked Romero up in the box of the ideological conflicts of his era. The climate today is quite different, as evidenced by the speeches of the Salvadoran left after it took power in 2009. Both President Mauricio Funes Cartagena and his successor, Salvador Sánchez Cerén, have spoken about Romero with respect, without denying his spiritual roots to make him a merely political banner as had happened in the past. Moreover, with the passage of time, more light has been shed on Romero and on his career, so that opinions about him have converged more. This is true even in El Salvador where the hatreds of the civil war had divided the country into factions that were opposed specifically over Romero's name. In his fatherland Romero is regarded today as an eminent figure in the nation's history, even by representatives of the political right that opposed him. Few people today still maintain that Romero was a Savonarola brainwashed by the Jesuit followers of liberation theology or by Communist revolutionaries.

Romero was accused of going beyond his responsibilities and engaging in politics. His authoritative statements had vehement political repercussions, but he compromised with no party or political faction, bound as he was by the Church's discipline in this matter. He was accused of fomenting violence, yet he suffered from the widespread violence in his country and tried to offer a remedy for it, condemning it wherever it came from. He was accused of being a subversive, while in reality he called for obedience to the laws and the Constitution. In them he found the norms that, if applied, would have brought justice to El Salvador. He was accused of being an extremist, and certainly he went outside the lines of conventional conduct. But he did so while proclaiming loudly and clearly the widespread need for justice. Romero would have liked to dedicate himself entirely to the *salus animarum* [salvation of souls]. The constant emergency situation prevented him from doing so. He wanted to be consistent with the many documents of Vatican II and of the papal magisterium that called him to illumine earthly realities with the Gospel. Because of the situation in which he lived and because of how he reacted to the actions of the civil authorities, he has been compared to Saint Stanislaus of Krakow. This eleventh-century saint was martyred by King Bolesław II for having criticized his cruel, unjust behavior toward his subjects. The comparison is appropriate.

Sometimes improper terms are used in reference to the martyrs. One is heroism, which not only misrepresents the sentiments of genuine martyrs but accentuates, so to speak, motivations based on character as opposed to spiritual motivations. Just as he did not feel that he was a prophet or a saint, Romero did not feel that he was a hero. Just think of his human fears, which drove him so often to consult physicians. Romero had no superhuman heroism, yet he did not want to give up being human, listening to his conscience, and respecting the dignity of the oppressed. He was unwilling to renounce his mission, even to save his life.

Another improper notion about martyrdom stresses the wickedness of the executioners, often against an ideological background, more than the testimony of faith. But martyrs, according to the Christian Tradition, are not protest symbols. Even Romero had no hatred for his enemies, from whose ranks his assassins came. He desired their conversion, not their chastisement. Romero did not think of his possible death as an act that would require reparation, much less retribution. He did not want his blood that might be shed to cry out for vengeance against someone, against an enemy, against a hostile ideology. Bloodshed and suffering ought to be situated in God's plan for the salvation of humanity. His death should help complete the sufferings of Christ in view of the redemption, to put it in the essential terms of Christian theology. Romero believed in this theology, spelled it out for the poor, for the victims of violence, and applied it also to himself from the moment he knew that he was close to a violent death.

Aside from his being well-liked by some and disliked by others, and apart from his successes and defeats, his strengths and his limitations, Romero was a man who considered it more important to be Christian than to safeguard his own life.

For Further Reading

The bibliography on Oscar Romero is very extensive. Here we will mention the essential works for the English-speaking reader. This volume is a significantly revised version of Roberto Morozzo della Rocca's, *Primero Dios: Vita di Oscar Romero* (Milan: Mondadori, 2005), which until now has been the only work based on the archives of the archdiocese of San Salvador and on Romero's personal papers. For editorial reasons, this volume dispenses with cumbersome footnotes, while utilizing the full range of documents. The interpretation of the subject is enhanced, thanks to the research conducted in the last decade, especially in relation to Oscar Romero's cause of beatification.

There are many biographies of Oscar Romero, three of which can be considered major works. The pioneer was the biography that appeared in the wake of his death, written by James R. Brockman, S.J., *The Word Remains: A Life of Oscar Romero* (Maryknoll, New York: Orbis Books, 1982). This book contains a few unpublished documents and very accurately reflects the heated atmosphere of the moment, although it has the related disadvantage of being too close to the events, which are narrated from a political perspective.[1] A biography by Jesús Delgado, Romero's former secretary, followed in 1986: *Oscar A. Romero: Biografía* (Madrid–San Salvador: Ediciones Paulinas–UCA Editores, 1986). It is an affectionate, first-hand account, with a Salvadoran sensibility, and extremely well documented.

Other biographies of Romero available in English are dated, such as those by Plácido Erdozaín, *Archbishop Romero, Martyr of Salvador* (Maryknoll, New York: Orbis Books, 1981), and one by the Irish journalist Dermot Keogh, *Romero, El Salvador's Martyr: A Study of the Tragedy of El Salvador* (Dublin: Dominican Publications, 1981). More recent popular biographies include those by Scott Wright, *Oscar Romero and the Communion of Saints* (Maryknoll, New York: Orbis Books, 2009), illustrated with over 100 photographs, and by Kevin Clarke, *Oscar Romero: Love Must Win Out* (Collegeville, Minnesota, 2014).

Attempts to situate Romero in a historical perspective and various interpretations of his significance within the Catholic Church are offered in two anthologies of essays: *Oscar Romero: Reflections on His Life and Writings*, edited by Marie Dennis et al. (Maryknoll, New York: Orbis Books, 2000), and *Monsignor Romero: A Bishop for the Third Millennium*, edited by Robert S. Pelton et al. (Notre Dame, Indiana: University of Notre Dame Press, 2004).

Reams of militant, apologetic, and often bombastic prose have been written about Romero (and some of it has been translated into

---

1. Father Brockman substantially rewrote the biography and republished it in 1989 as *Romero: A Life*; a slightly updated edition appeared in 2005. —*Trans.*

English). It has served as the basis for the spread of the theological myth of Romero, the political prophet. This myth originated in the interpretations popularized by Jon Sobrino in numerous essays celebrating the archbishop and martyr, which were then collected (in Spanish) in his anthology *Monseñor Romero* (San Salvador: UCA Editores, 1989).

To approach the figure of Romero directly, it is advisable to read his personal diary: Archbishop Oscar Romero, *A Shepherd's Diary*, translated by Irene B. Hodgson (Cincinnati, Ohio: St. Anthony Messenger Press / Montreal: Novalis, 1993), and the collection of his homilies published in San Salvador by Publicaciones Pastorales del Arzobispado from 1980 to 1989, in seven volumes, under the title of *Su pensamiento*. A selection is available in English: *Voice of the Voiceless: The Four Pastoral Letters and Other Statements*, translated by Michael J. Walsh (Maryknoll, New York: Orbis Books, 1985). Various homilies by Romero, taken from the seven-volume series, are available in Spanish online at several websites dedicated to Romero, starting with the official website of the Archdiocese of San Salvador (www.arzobispadosansalvador.org/). There the entire corpus of Romero's writings and speeches, running to thousands of pages, has been digitized (homilies, diary, pastoral letters, articles in periodicals and newspapers).

About the Author

Roberto Morozzo della Rocca (b. 1955) teaches modern history at Roma Tre University. He specializes in the relations between religions and nations and also in those between modernity and the sacred—a subject on which he has published a dozen volumes, some of which have been translated into various languages. Among his most recent publications are *Passaggio a Oriente: La modernità e l'Europa ortodossa* [*Passage to the East: Modernity and Orthodox Europe*] (Brescia, 2012) and *Tra Est e Ovest: Agostino Casaroli diplomatico vaticano* [*Between East and West: Agostino Casaroli, Vatican Diplomat*] (Cinisello Balsamo, 2014). Since the 1990s he has been conducting research into the political and religious history of Latin America, in particular the figure of Oscar Romero. His findings are included in the anthology *Oscar Romero: Un vescovo centroamerica-*

no tra guerra fredda e rivoluzione [*Oscar Romero: A Central American Bishop between Cold War and Revolution*] (Milan, Cinisello Balsamo, 2002) and in an initial scholarly biographical volume entitled *Primero Dios: Vita di Oscar Romero* [*God First: The Life of Oscar Romero*] (Milan, Cinisello Balsamo, 2005), after which he was invited to collaborate as an expert on the process for the canonization of the bishop and martyr. The present biography of Romero is therefore the result of many years of study.